DHARAM P. GHAI

taxation for development

A CASE STUDY OF UGANDA

East African Studies 23

Taxation for Development

A Case Study of Uganda

Written under the auspices of
The East African Institute of Social Research,
Kampala

Taxation for Development

A CASE STUDY OF UGANDA

(by) DHARAM P. GHAI

East African Publishing House

EAST AFRICAN PUBLISHING HOUSE
Uniafric House, Koinange Street
P.O. Box 30571, Nairobi

First published 1966

Copyright © East African Institute of Social Research,
Kampala, 1966

For my Parents

*Made and printed in Kenya
by Kenya Litho Ltd., Cardiff Road, Nairobi*

Contents

CONTENTS

TABLES

TABLES

DIAGRAMS AND CHARTS

PREFACE

This monograph is a slightly altered version of a dissertation presented to Yale University in partial fulfilment of the requirements for the degree of doctor of philosophy.

In the course of preparing this study I have received help, in one form or another, from a large number of persons. It is not possible to mention them all by name. However, I should like to acknowledge publicly my debt to certain individuals who have been especially helpful. I am grateful to Professor P. W. Bell for giving me a term off from teaching responsibilities in 1964 to enable me to concentrate on my research. For their help in statistical computations I am indebted to W. Kizza, Z. Velji, K. Dawood and Anne Cooper. I owe a special word of thanks to Mrs. Winifred da Silva for her able and cheerful secretarial assistance. I have further benefited from the valuable comments on the draft manuscript made by Lady Hicks, Professor A. R. Prest, Professor J. F. Due, Professor Challis Hall, Professor Lloyd Reynolds, Dr. C. R. Frank, Dr. B. Van Arkadie and Dr. R. H. Green. I am deeply indebted to all of them.

My greatest intellectual debt, however, is to Professor Paul G. Clark who, over a period of two years, has contributed more to the fruition of this study than he probably realizes. His arrival in Kampala as Director of the Economic Development Research Project at the East African Institute of Social Research, Makerere, gave a tremendous boost to economic research in East Africa, and those of us who were privileged to work under him are deeply conscious of the many ways in which he influenced the substance and form of our work.

Finally, I must express my debt to my wife Neela who has been a source of encouragement to me throughout the preparation of this study; and a word of apology to my little daughter, Kamini, who learnt, though not without vigorous protests, to play by herself in the evenings.

February 1966

Dharam P. Ghai
Economic Growth Centre
Yale University

Chapter I

INCOME ELASTICITY AS A TAX CRITERION IN DEVELOPING COUNTRIES

I Introduction

There is now widespread agreement among economists as to the criteria to be used in judging the efficiency of different taxes. Most writers on Public Finance would advocate the following set of criteria in evaluating different taxes[1]:

(a) Effect on the allocation and supply of resources.

(b) Efficiency in securing economic stabilization.

(c) Effect on equity.

(d) Administrative efficiency.

There has been relatively little systematic discussion of the appropriate criteria for the evaluation of the tax systems of underdeveloped countries. In general, it tends to be assumed that the same set of criteria should be used in underdeveloped as in advanced economies, though the weight to be attached to any single criterion will vary from one country to another. The main purpose of this chapter is to advance income elasticity as an additional tax criterion and to work out some of its important implications in the context of underdeveloped economies. This criterion is implicitly included in the conventional criteria: the more income elastic the tax system, the greater its efficiency in securing economic stabilization. Some of the built-in stabilizers have the effect of enhancing the income elasticity of fiscal systems and hence their income stabilizing properties. But an elastic tax system is only one of the ways of securing stabilization.

Before proceeding further, it is essential to provide a working definition of the income elasticity tax criterion. For purposes of this study a tax system is considered elastic if, with an unchanged tax structure, the incremental tax revenue/national income ratio is greater than the average tax revenue/national income ratio. The elasticity of a given tax will, therefore, be determined by the relationships among (a) marginal rate of taxation, (b) average rate of

---

1. See, for instance, two important works on Public Finance published in recent years: R. A. Musgrave, *The Theory of Public Finance* (McGraw-Hill Book Co., Inc., New York, 1959), p. 5; and A. R. Prest, *Public Finance*, (Wiedenfeld and Nicolson, London, 1960), p. 27. Although they employ different terminology, both Musgrave and Prest are in complete agreement on the criteria to be used for evaluating taxes.

taxation, (c) marginal share of tax base in national income, (d) average share of tax base in national income.[2] The income elasticity of a tax system or, of a group of taxes, will be equal to the weighted average of the elasticities of component taxes, the weights being their respective yields.[3] Therefore, any given tax system will be elastic provided the weighted average of the elasticities of its component taxes is greater than one.

II Advantages of an Income Elastic Tax System in Underdeveloped Countries.

It is only recently that economists have started to recognize the importance of an elastic tax structure for developing countries.[4] The case for an elastic tax system in developing countries, however, does not rest on the stabilizing property of such a system, as in the advanced economies. In fact, as we shall see below, this property of a tax system may have several undesirable consequences for an underdeveloped country.

The case for having an income elastic fiscal system rests rather on the well-recognized tendency in most underdeveloped countries for public expenditure to show a continuous upward trend, not only absolutely but also relative to other expenditures i.e. the ratio of public expenditure to national income tends to show a long-run upward trend[5]. It is easy to explain this upward trend. In most

---

2. See Footnote 1, p. 67 for a mathematical formulation of this definition.

3. W. Vickrey, "Some Limits to the Income Elasticity of Income Tax Yield", *Review of Economics and Statistics* (1949, May) p. 140-144. This proposition may be proved as follows:
   Where e′, e″ and e are the elasticities of the components and tax system respectively, and t′, t″ and T the yields of the components and the tax system, and Y the national income,

$$e = \frac{Y}{T} \cdot \frac{dT}{dY}$$

$$= \left(\frac{Y}{t' + t''}\right) \cdot \frac{d(t' + t'')}{dY}$$

$$= \frac{1}{t' + t''} \left(\frac{Ydt'}{dY} + \frac{Ydt''}{dY}\right)$$

$$= \frac{t'e' + t''e''}{t' + t''}$$

4. In this connection, see R. J. Chelliah, *Fiscal Policy in Underdeveloped Countries*, (George Allen and Unwin, London, 1960) p. 66; A. R. Prest, *Public Finance in Underdeveloped Countries* (Weidenfeld and Nicolson, London, 1962) pp. 25, 26. G. S. Sahota, *Indian Tax Structure and Economic Development* (Asia Publishing House, Bombay, 1961).

5. United Nations, *Economic Bulletin for Africa* Vol. 1, No. 2 (Addis Ababa, June 1961): "Public Finance in African Countries" Table 14, p. 24. See also *Economic Survey of Asia and the Far East, 1960* (U.N., Bangkok, 1961) p. 45.

underdeveloped countries, for a variety of reasons, the share of public investment in total investment has risen sharply in recent years. There has also been a distinct rise in the share of government current services in national income, mainly due to popular pressures for increased social services. There are strong reasons to believe that this upward trend is likely to continue, and indeed to intensify, for some years to come[6]. It is, therefore, essential that the public revenue should increase *pari passu* if strong inflationary pressures on the economy are to be avoided. We may distinguish here five important sources of public revenue: (*a*) Fees, departmental earnings etc., (*b*) Taxation, (*c*) Internal borrowing from the public, (*d*) Credit creation or borrowing from the Central Bank, (*e*) Foreign loans and grants. The scope for increasing revenue from sources (*a*) and (*c*) is rather limited in most developing countries, and this is especially true of the East African countries in their present circumstances[7]. Although foreign loans and grants may be expected to increase in future, considerations of debt servicing and restrictions on the use of aid to purchases from the donor country greatly limit the role of foreign aid in solving the revenue problems of the developing countries. In any case, the amount of foreign assistance forthcoming is determined by economic as well as a host of non-economic factors, and cannot therefore be relied upon with any degree of certainty for financing public expenditure. East African countries which have been fortunate in the amount of foreign aid they have been able to attract, are finding domestic finance an important constraint on the implementation of their development plans[8]. Many developing countries, especially in Asia and Latin America, have made liberal use of credit creation to finance government expenditure, which has generated strong inflationary pressures in the economy. In East Africa, credit creation in the orthodox sense i.e. borrowing from the Central Bank, has not been possible owing to the lack of a fully developed monetary system with a

---

6. A. R. Prest, *op. cit.*, pp. 14-20.

7. For the difficulties in the way of internal borrowing from the public in developing countries see Prest, *op. cit.*, pp. 104, 105; and R. N. Tripathy, *Public Finance in Underdeveloped Countries*, (The World Press Private Ltd., Calcutta, 1964) pp. 175-178.

8. For the viewpoint that finance, as distinct from foreign exchange and domestic savings, is likely to be the most important constraint on development in East Africa see P. G. Clark, "Foreign Aid, Domestic Finance and the Development Plan" *Economic Development Research Project* Paper No. 45 (East African Institute of Social Research, Kampala, 1964), mimeo.

Central Bank.[9] The East African Governments have now decided to replace the present Currency Board system by separate Central Banks in Kenya, Uganda and Tanzania. There is little doubt that with the establishment of Central Banks, the scope for financing public expenditure through credit creation will be greatly increased. But even here, the basically agricultural nature of the economies and the existence of high marginal propensity to import will severely restrict the use of deficit financing. It is, therefore, doubtful whether credit creation by itself could provide the necessary finance without leading to inflation and balance of payments difficulties, as in many Latin American and Asian countries. We must, therefore, conclude that the main burden of finding additional revenue must rest on taxation[10]. In order for this to be possible, the tax structure must be income elastic, which will enable the public sector to appropriate a growing share of the marginal increases in income. This is the most important reason for ensuring a long-run income elasticity of the tax system. If a country possesses an inelastic tax system, rising public expenditure could either be financed by continuous credit creation with all the attendant dangers of inflation and balance of payments crises, or by annual upward revisions of the existing tax rates. The latter will have a bad psychological effect on incentives to save, work and invest, and will be administratively difficult and politically unpopular; lastly, piecemeal tinkering with the tax system to secure more revenue will make it more difficult to fashion a consistent fiscal policy for growth. Some or all of these effects may be avoided by having a built-in flexibility in the tax system.

Another advantage of a flexible tax system, as noted above, is its efficacy as an instrument of stabilization. An elastic tax system will impart an element of stability to private incomes in the economy. This function may be important as underdeveloped primary producing countries are especially susceptible to violent, short-run fluctuations[11].

Lastly, on the assumption that increased tax revenue is used productively in the fulfilment of soundly conceived development plans, it can be argued that an elastic tax structure will help

---

9. The mode of operation of the Currency Board type of monetary system is described in W. T. Newlyn and A. Rowan, *Money and Banking in British Colonial Africa*, (Oxford: the Clarendon Press, 1954): and D. C. Mead, "Monetary Analysis—an East African Case Study", *Yale Economic Essays*, Vol. 3, No. 1, Spring, 1963.

10. This conclusion receives further support in the case of Uganda from quantitative data presented in Chapter VI, p. 118

11. This is particularly true of Uganda: see Chapter II.

accelerate the process of economic growth by stepping up the rate of capital formation.

III Possible Disadvantages of an Income Elastic Tax System

There are several alleged disadvantages associated with an elastic tax structure. We must, therefore, consider whether it is possible to remove them while preserving the income elasticity of the tax system.

In the first place, in the very process of stabilizing private incomes, a flexible tax system destabilizes public revenue. This necessary property of a flexible tax system is recognized and accepted in developed economies. In developing countries, faced with a choice between stabilization of private income and public revenue, it is not at all clear as to where the choice ought to lie. While fluctuating private incomes may create a state of uncertainty, extreme fluctuations in public revenue, especially in countries where sizeable deficit finance is either not possible or not desirable, may jeopardize their development efforts. It is, therefore, desirable to ensure a reasonable degree of stability in public revenue. How can this be done without abandoning the flexibility of the tax system?

In theory, there are four ways of preserving long-run elasticity of the tax system while ensuring short-run stability of public revenue and expenditure.

1. *Counter-cyclical Fiscal Policy*

This method, which in some ways is the most attractive, works by insulating public expenditure from fluctuations in public revenue. This can be done by building up budget surpluses in good years and running them down in bad years so as to ensure a reasonable degree of stability in public expenditure[12]. It will be noticed that this proposal does not eliminate fluctuations in public revenue but merely prevents them from generating similar fluctuations in expenditure. Such a policy has been successfully, if perhaps unconsciously, pursued in several African countries in the post-war period[13].

The drawbacks of this kind of policy are well known. First, there is the difficulty of distinguishing between the trend and short-

12. A similar proposal is put forward by R. Nurkse in "Trade Fluctuations and Buffer Policies of Low-income Countries", *Kyklos* (Vol. 11, 1958) pp.141-154.
13. United Nations, *Economic Bulletin for Africa, op. cit.*, p. 11.

run fluctuations in prices of primary product exports which are the basic cause of instability in national income and public revenue in most developing countries. Even if this difficulty could be overcome, most governments find it hard to resist the temptation to spend extravagantly in good years. Lastly, a necessary condition for the successful implementation of this policy is the existence of large surpluses of funds accumulated in the past and/or a boom in commodity prices at a time when the decision is taken to pursue such counter-cyclical policies.

We may, therefore, conclude that despite its apparent attraction, a counter-cyclical policy of this kind is unlikely to succeed in underdeveloped countries except in unusually favourable circumstances such as those obtaining during the Korean War.

2. *Averaging of Income*

This proposal involves an application of the technique for stabilizing incomes in primary producing areas to the public finances of these countries. Short-run fluctuations in public revenue caused by corresponding fluctuations in income may be smoothed out if the basis of income taxes is changed from the current income to a moving average of, say, three years. This will impart an element of stability to government revenue without destroying the long-run elasticity of the tax system. Nor is this suggestion as novel as it might appear at first; the principle of averaging income is already applied in a number of countries to incomes which are especially susceptible to fluctuations. The proposal outlined here amounts to an application of this principle to all taxable incomes in countries where these are subject to considerable fluctuations.

The results achieved by this proposal are, however, likely to be small, as revenue from income taxes constitutes a relatively small proportion of total tax revenue in most underdeveloped countries. Moreover, this proposal suffers from the disadvantage of being administratively inconvenient and costly. In most underdeveloped countries, where the machinery of tax assessment and collection is already either overstrained or plain inefficient it may be doubted whether the additional stability obtained in government revenue is worth the price of considerable administrative costs. Furthermore, greater stability in revenue from income taxes will imply a greater instability in personal and corporate disposable income, and hence in revenue from outlay taxes through its effect on consumption. However, the net effect is likely to be an improvement in the stability of total tax revenue, as consumption tends to be more stable than income, in underdeveloped as in advanced countries.

3. *Shift of Emphasis Towards Outlay Taxes*

This proposal is based on the assumption that consumption tends to be more stable than income in the short-run, and therefore, a greater reliance on outlay taxes will make for a more stable tax revenue. However, a greater reliance on outlay taxes need not imply a lower income elasticity of tax system in the long-run, as the ratio of consumption to income has been shown in many countries to be constant over long periods[14]. A tax system may be made elastic by relatively high rates of income tax on marginal increases in income and/or by relatively heavy taxation of commodities with a high income elasticity of demand. With a given degree of elasticity of the tax system, the required revenue may be raised either through an emphasis on income taxes or outlay taxes. The proposal outlined here argues for a shift of emphasis toward outlay taxes in order to bring about greater stability of tax receipts.

Most of the underdeveloped countries already rely heavily on indirect, outlay taxes[15]. The scope for further increased reliance on outlay taxes may therefore be rather limited in most underdeveloped countries. Besides, rates on outlay taxes will have to be devised carefully in order to avoid a regressive tax structure. Despite these qualifications, there are several low-income countries where there is considerable scope for improving the short-run stability of tax receipts through greater reliance on outlay taxes.

4. *'Kinked' Tax Rates*

It is possible to devise a tax system which is income elastic only in the upward but not in the downward direction. This can be achieved by altering rates of income as well as outlay taxes in the upward direction when income falls in any given period. This method achieves stability and buoyancy of revenue simultaneously by raising the effective average rate of taxation over a given period.

The drawbacks of this proposal are that it assumes considerable predictive ability on the part of public authorities, is discretionary rather than automatic, is politically impracticable and will involve constant adjustment of rates with all its disadvantages—

---

14. While most of the investigations have drawn on data from the advanced countries, there is no *a priori* reason to believe that the position is different in underdeveloped countries. It may, however, be argued that in underdeveloped countries the public policy ought to aim at *reducing* the ratio of consumption to income so as to step up the rate of capital accumulation.

15. W. A. Lewis and A. Martin, "Patterns of Public Revenue and Expenditure", *Manchester School of Economic and Social Studies*, Vol. 24 (September 1956) pp. 203-244.

uncertainty, inequity, etc. It would, therefore, appear that this proposal is inferior to the ones suggested above.

To summarize our discussion in this section, we may say that short-run stability of public revenue can be secured, without sacrificing long-run elasticity, through a variety of methods, but the actual application of these methods presents considerable practical difficulties. Nevertheless, a partial application of proposals 1, 2, and 3 may go some way towards alleviating the worst effects of sharp fluctuations in revenue.

Income Elasticity Criterion and Incentives

Another important disadvantage of an elastic tax system is alleged to be its disincentive effects on the supply of resources such as risk, effort and savings[16]. We must separate out two aspects of this question: (a) the relevance of the tax base to various incentives; (b) effects of different rate structures on incentives.

For all practical purposes, the two relevant bases for taxation in underdeveloped countries are income and outlay. A tax on capital is unlikely to bring much revenue, but is certain to impose a heavy administrative burden on the machinery of tax collection. A proportional income tax will have the usual income and substitution effects on the incentives to work, save, invest and take risks. It is now generally recognized that in theory at least it is not possible to say whether the imposition of a proportional income tax will diminish or increase the supply of these resources: the empirical data are too scarce to permit the testing of any hypothesis. Yet there is a persistent feeling that income taxes have adverse effects on these incentives. Certainly the public debate on taxes is conducted on the assumption that income taxes have harmful effects on incentives. If this is true of proportional taxes, it is true *a fortiori* of progressive taxes, which will in all cases intensify the disincentive effects of the former.

Partial taxes on outlay, such as selective customs and excise duties, will lead to the substitution of non-taxed for taxed goods and services. Apart from that, their effect on incentives will tend to be in the same direction as those of a general consumption tax. In contrast to income taxes which tend to discriminate against future in favour of present consumption, outlay taxes are neutral as between present and future consumption[17]. Their effect on the

---

16. A. R. Prest, *op. cit.*, p. 26.
17. Musgrave, *op. cit.*, p. 261.

supply of effort will depend on the relationship between present consumption, future consumption and leisure. Work effort will be higher under the consumption than the income tax if present consumption and work are rivals, while future consumption and work are complementary; and it will be higher under the income tax if these relations are reversed[18].

As for the effect on aggregate investment, a consumption tax will enable the economy to devote a larger proportion of income to capital formation through its relatively favourable effect on savings. It is more difficult to be certain about the relative effects of income and consumption taxes on risk-taking. The general consensus appears to be that it is difficult to say in the abstract which type of tax has more favourable effects on risk-taking[19].

We may, therefore, conclude that on grounds of incentives, consumption appears to be a preferable tax base. It is difficult to make a more positive statement in view of the tentative nature of a good deal of analysis in this field and also in view of the many highly restrictive assumptions that have to be made for the validation of any definite conclusions.

However, the incentive argument often advanced against an income elastic tax system refers to the rate structure and not to the tax base. We have seen above that an elastic tax system implies that the marginal rates of taxation are higher than the average. In general, the higher the marginal rate of taxation, the greater the disincentive effects of taxation. The exact force of this argument will, however, depend on the actual circumstances prevailing in a country. In countries where most of the high income recipients are not free to vary the supply of their effort, as in Uganda, the disincentive effects of high marginal rates of taxes will be minimal. The disincentive effects on the supply of saving may be reduced or eliminated by such devices as an increased emphasis on outlay taxes and partial or complete exemption of desirable investment from taxation[20]. Without going into further details, it may be stated

---

18. *ibid.*, p. 249.

19. Musgrave and Domar have shown that with full loss offsets income tax may under certain circumstances even increase the amount of risk undertaken; see, E. D. Domar and R. A. Musgrave "Proportional Income Taxation and Risk-taking", *Quarterly Journal of Economics*, Vol. LXIII (May, 1944) pp. 388-422. N. Kaldor in his book, *An Expenditure Tax* (George Allen and Unwin, London, 1955) p.119, has argued that under certain conditions, an expenditure tax may be more conducive to risk-taking. For a different viewpoint see A. R. Prest, *Public Finance*, p. 48.

20. *Chelliah, op. cit.*, pp. 71-81 has proposed a detailed scheme for the exemption of approved investments from income taxation. See also *Report of the Taxation Enquiry Commission*, 1953-54, Vol. II (New Delhi, Government of India Press, 1955).

here that an imaginative use of fiscal policy can remove serious disincentive effects of a tax system while preserving its basic flexibility.

Income Elasticity Criterion and Equity

It is now generally recognized that equity demands that persons should be taxed according to their ability to pay, which in turn is usually interpreted to imply a progressive tax structure. In order for the tax receipts to be sensitive to increases in income it is essential that taxes on income should be progressive and that the commodities with a high income elasticity of demand should be taxed at relatively high rates. Since such commodities are usually non-necessities, an elastic structure of outlay taxes will not conflict with the equity criterion. However, there may be some essential commodities which have a high income elasticity of demand at a certain level of income; it would be desirable to exempt them from indirect taxes in order to prevent a conflict between income elasticity and equity criteria. As far as income taxes are concerned, both equity and income elasticity criteria require a progressive tax structure.

Finally, it may be argued that the income elasticity criterion would make for a relative expansion of the public sector. It is not the intention here to enter into the wider controversy on the role of public versus private enterprise in the economic development of underdeveloped areas. Suffice it to say that there is a large measure of agreement among economists working in underdeveloped countries that the quickening of the process of development will in most cases require a substantial increase in the activities and importance of the public sector in underdeveloped countries. Certainly the governments of developing countries are determined to increase their share in the total investment undertaken. In these circumstances, it is useful to consider how tax structure might be reformed to contribute to the fulfilment of this important objective.

One other point needs to be discussed. Can we say anything about the optimum degree of income elasticity of the tax structure and about the optimum proportion of tax receipts to national income? There can be no general answer to either of these two questions; it will depend on the particular circumstances of the country in question and will be influenced by a large number of factors such as the seriousness of the disincentive effects of a steeply progressive tax structure, the efficiency and productivity of public expenditure, the vitality of the private sector, and the stage of economic development of the country. Therefore a precise answer to the questions posed above will require a detailed study of the economic   characteristics, social and cultural institutions, and prevailing standards of tax administration and compliance of any given country. We may, however, hazard the generalization that most underdeveloped countries have inelastic tax structures and "could increase the proportion of their national income taken by taxation without unduly disturbing the economy and perhaps even with positive gains in the face of inflationary pressures"[21]. Thus even though we cannot provide a quantitative answer, our qualitative judgement is that most underdeveloped countries could benefit from a greater flexibility of their fiscal systems.

IV. Conclusion

The main purpose of the present study is to devise a method for calculating the income elasticity of the Uganda tax structure and to suggest reforms designed to enhance its income elasticity, while avoiding serious adverse effects on incentives to work, to save and to take risks. This topic has received relatively little attention in the literature on Public Finance. Most of the work in the developed countries has been concerned with the calculation of the built-in flexibility of individual taxes, especially of income tax[22]. Recently two interesting attempts have been made to calculate the income elasticity of the tax system as a whole in India and Pakistan[23]. Both these studies compute income elasticities of individual taxes as well as of the tax system as a whole on the basis of tax receipts over a number of years. However, no attempt is made in either of these studies to relate tax revenue to economic growth, or to make projections of tax revenue, except in a very mechanical manner.

---

21. United Nations, *Taxes and Fiscal Policy in Underdeveloped Countries* (New York: United Nations, 1954).

22. The following may be cited as examples of this kind of work: L. J. Cohen, "An Empirical Measurement of the Built-in Flexibility of the Individual Income Tax", *American Economic Review*, Vol. XLIX (May 1959) pp. 532-541; E. Cary Brown and R. J. Kruizenga, "Income Sensitivity of a Simple Personal Income Tax", *Review of Economics and Statistics*, Vol. XLI (August, 1959) pp. 260-269; L. J. Cohen, "A More Recent Measurement of the Built-in Flexibility of the Individual Income Tax", *National Tax Journal*, (1960). J. A. Pechman, "Yield of the Individual Income Tax During a Recession", in *Policies to Combat Depression*, National Bureau of Economic Research (Princeton University Press, 1956); A. R. Prest, "The Sensitivity of the Yield of Personal Income Tax in the U.K.", *Economic Journal*, Vol. LXXII (September, 1962) pp. 576-596; R. E. Bretherton, "The Sensitivity of Taxes to Fluctuations of Trade", *Econometrica*, Vol. V. (1937) pp. 171-183.

23. G. S. Sahota, *Indian Tax Structure and Economic Development* (Bombay: Asia Publishing House, 1961) and A. H. M. Nuruddin Chowdhury, "The Predictability and the Flexibility of Tax Revenues in Pakistan", *The Pakistan Development Review* Vol. III (1963).

The present study, like the studies by Sahota and Nuruddin Chowdhury, attempts to measure the sensitivity of tax receipts to changes in income in the past; but the main emphasis is placed on the fiscal effects of different patterns and rates of economic growth. Furthermore, this study attempts to develop a method for making projections of tax revenue. It is hoped that by highlighting the exact relationship between tax revenue and structure of the economy, this study will draw attention to the fiscal implications of structural changes in the economy, and thus improve the consistency and feasibility of development plans in underdeveloped countries.

The next chapter which gives an outline of the main characteristics of the Uganda economy, and of its fiscal system, is followed by an analysis of the growth and changes in the composition of tax revenue in the post-war period. The last three chapters are taken up with a discussion of the income elasticity of the current tax structure, projection of tax revenue over the next eight years and suggestions designed to improve the responsiveness of the Uganda tax system to increases in income.

Chapter II

→THE ECONOMY AND THE TAX STRUCTURE IN UGANDA

I. Characteristics of the Uganda Economy[1]

Uganda offers an example *par excellence* of an underdeveloped country; its economy answers perfectly to the text-book description of a low-income country. In 1963 with an estimated population of over 7 million and total gross domestic product (G.D.P.) of £176.1 million, output per head amounted to £24.5 per annum, which is among the lowest per capita income figures in the world. Table 1 presents some of the essential information on the Uganda economy.

TABLE I
Structure of the Economy: 1963

		£m.	% of G.D.P.
(a)	Total Gross Domestic Product	176.1	—
(b)	Monetary Economy	128.8	73.1
(c)	Non-monetary economy	47.3	26.9

Monetary Economy		% of Monetary G.D.P.
Agriculture, including forestry, fishing etc. ..	65.4	50.9
Mining and quarrying	2.8	2.2
Manufacturing	6.8	5.3
Electricity, Transport & Communications	9.0	6.9
Construction	3.5	2.7
Commerce	18.4	14.2
Government	7.0	5.5
Miscellaneous	15.9	12.4
Total exports[1]	59.7	46.4
Cotton and Coffee exports	41.5	32.2
Total imports[1]	37.9	29.4
Gross Capital Formation	19.4	15.1
Total Central Government expenditure[2]	35.5	27.6

Notes: 1. Total exports and imports are exclusive of re-exports, but include exports to and imports from the other East African countries. As both exports to and imports from outside East Africa are valued at Mombasa, this has the effect of underestimating imports and over-estimating exports by a margin equivalent to the transport costs between Mombasa and the Uganda border.

2. Expenditure for the financial year 1963/64, including Appropriations-in-Aid.

Source: Abstracted from *Background to the Budget* 1965-66, Uganda Government (Ministry of Finance, May 1965).

---

1. For a fuller discussion of the characteristics of the East African economies see B. Van Arkadie, "The Structure of the Economies", *Economic Development Research Project Paper No. 61* (East African Institute of Social Research, Kampala, 1964) mimeo.

It will be seen from the above table that a high proportion of
G.D.P.—very nearly 27%—is derived from subsistence activities,
and that agriculture alone accounts for well over 50% of monetary
G.D.P. Unlike many other African countries, Uganda does not
possess large mineral resources; the only important mineral export is
copper, which has amounted to £3-4m. per annum in recent years.
Despite its rapid growth in the post-war period, manufacturing still
forms just over 5% of monetary G.D.P. Apart from cotton ginning,
coffee curing and other food processing factories, manufacturing
consists of beer, soap, copper mining, cement, fertilizers, cotton
textiles and steel rolling operations. The most important influence
on the level of national income is export earnings, which amounted
to about £60m in 1963, or over 46% of monetary G.D.P. A
great majority of these exports—about 70%—consists of cotton
and coffee, grown on small farms by a million peasants scattered all
over the country. Other important exports are copper, tea and
animal feeding stuffs; while sugar and cotton piece-goods are exported to Kenya and Tanzania.

Imports consist for the most part of machinery and equipment,
manufactured consumer goods and fuel. Gross capital formation,
of which about 60% is usually undertaken by the Public Sector,
amounted to over 15% of the monetary G.D.P. in 1963. Finally,
government expenditure, amounting to over 27% of monetary
G.D.P., has an important influence on the level of economic activity
in the country.

The vast majority of Africans are self-employed, deriving their
livelihood from cultivation and cattle-rearing; in 1963 wage and salary
earners, numbering just over 208,000, constituted less than 6% of
adult Uganda Africans. Non-Africans, mostly Asians of Indo-
Pakistani origin, though small in number, play a crucial role in the
economy; in 1962-63, for example, Europeans and Asians, constitut-
ing slightly less than 1.4% of the total population, received about
26% of monetary incomes[2]. They provide a high proportion of
the middle and high-level manpower in Uganda. Their contribution is especially noticeable in commerce and industry which are
largely dependent on non-African capital and entrepreneurial skills.

Another important feature of the economy is its close integra-

---

2. D. P. Ghai, "Some Aspects of Income Distribution in East Africa",
The East African Economic Review (December, 1965).

tion with the other East African countries[3]. Kenya, Uganda and Tanzania form a common market, with a largely common external tariff, more or less free internal trade,[4] and freedom of mobility of labour and capital. They have a common currency and a common monetary system. However, the three governments have now decided to operate separate currencies and Central Banks as from some time in 1966. In the fiscal field, some of the most important taxes such as Income Tax and Customs and Excise duties are similar in the three countries. In addition to all this, there is an impressive range of services which are operated jointly on an East African basis; these include railways and harbours, posts and tele-communications, airways, revenue collection, research and statistical services and higher education. Clearly such a high degree of economic integration has important consequences for the Uganda economy. However, our main concern here is with the tax system, and we discuss in a later section some of the fiscal implications of Uganda's participation in the East African Common Market.

Before concluding this brief survey of the Uganda economy, it is necessary to say something about the recent experience and future prospects for growth in this country[5]. Table II shows the growth of monetary G.D.P., exports, imports, government expenditure and gross capital formation in the post-war period. It will be noticed that the Uganda economy enjoyed a phenomenally fast rate of growth between 1946 and 1952. The growth in monetary income slowed down considerably after 1952, while there was a virtual stagnation between 1957 and 1962. The year 1963 saw a resumption of rapid economic expansion. As Table II shows, the key to an understanding of the Uganda economy is to be sought in the behaviour of export earnings. Chart I shows the changes in total export earnings alongside with annual changes in monetary

---

3. For a fuller discussion of the various aspects of economic integration in East Africa see the following: *East Africa: Report of the Economic and Fiscal Commission* (Cmnd. 1279), (London; Her Majesty's Stationery Office, 1961); J. S. Nye, "East African Economic Integration"· *Journal of Modern African Studies*, Vol. 1, No. 4 (1963) pp. 475-502; B. F. Massell, *East African Economic Union: An Evaluation and Some Implications for Policy* (Santa Monica, Rand, 1963); D. Ghai, "Territorial Distribution of Benefits and Costs of the East African Common Market". *The East African Economic Review*, Vol. II, No. 1. (June 1964) pp. 29-40; *Federation in East Africa: Opportunities and Problems*, edited by P. Robson and C. Leys (Nairobi: Oxford University Press, 1965). P. Ndegwa, *The Common Market and Development in East Africa* (Nairobi: East African Publishing House, 1965).

4. Recently there has been some modification to the principle of free internal trade; see *Kampala Agreement* (Dar es Salaam, 1964).

5. For a detailed discussion of the growth in the post-war period see D. P. Ghai, "The Growth of Money Incomes in East Africa: 1946-60", in *East Africa: Past and Present*, edited by D. Stenning (Paris: Editions Presence Africaine, 1964).

CHART 1

Annual Fluctuations in monetary
G.D.P. and Export Earnings

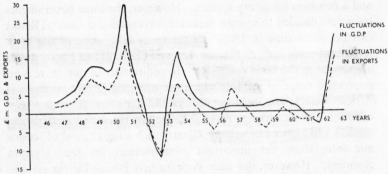

G.D.P. in the post-war period. A very close correlation between these two variables brings out the crucial fact that the most important influence on the growth of the Uganda economy has been changes in export earnings. The extraordinarily rapid growth of domestic product from 1946 to 1951 is closely paralleled by an equally rapid increase in export earnings, caused mainly by a big rise in the prices of her two major exports—cotton and coffee. Likewise, the relative stagnation of monetary income between 1955 and 1962 is paralleled by a levelling off of export earnings, which in turn was caused by a severe deterioration of terms of trade; Uganda's export price index fell by 50% between 1954 and 1962.[6] The rapid growth in 1963 was wholly due to a sharp rise in export earnings, caused by a substantial increase in coffee prices and output.

The other major influence on monetary G.D.P.—government expenditure—has had the effect, on the whole, of moderating fluctuations in the economy generated by the volatility of export earnings. In the early post-war years, although the total government expenditure increased very rapidly, government revenue from taxation increased even more rapidly; the budgetary surpluses coupled with the surpluses built up by the cotton and coffee marketing boards had the effect of restraining expansionary forces generated by rising export earnings. The steady upward trend of government expenditure in the period 1955 to 1962, made possible in the main by running down surpluses accumulated in early post-war years,

---

6. Nils Ramm-Ericson, "The Price Movements in East Africa's Exports", *Economic and Statistical Review*, No. 11 (June 1964). According to the Paasche Index the fall was 50 per cent, while the Fisher Ideal Index gives a fall of 40 per cent.

has partially offset the depressing effect of stagnation in export earnings, and has helped the economy avoid a decline in G.D.P.

It is, therefore, clear from the above account that in the short-run, international forces determining the supply of and demand for commodities exported by Uganda—principally cotton and coffee—will have a decisive influence on the rate of growth of the economy. Efforts are now being made in Uganda to diversify the country's export base as well as to push forward with a vigorous programme of industrialization. The success of these efforts themselves will be closely dependent on the future prices of Uganda's main exports.

TABLE II
Growth of the Uganda Economy : 1946-63
£ million

Year	Monetary G.D.P.[1]	Exports[2]	Government Expenditure[3]	Gross Capital Formation	Retained Imports[4]
1946	21.4	11.6		N.A.	6.1
1947	24.6	13.6	4.5	N.A.	7.5
1948	30.3	17.1	6.5	N.A	10.4
1949	42.8	26.6	6.7	N.A	14.0
1950	54.3	32.9	8.0	N.A.	17.8
1951	83.8	51.5	12.4	N.A.	23.8
1952	88.3	51.0	16.0	N.A.	26.1
1953	76.3	40.4	17.4	N.A.	28.6
1954	92.8	48.1	19.1	18.6	28.0
1955	102.0	49.8	22.0	23.2	37.5
1956	102.8	44.9	23.5	21.8	32.2
1957	109.4	51.2	24.8	20.4	34.4
1958	105.9	51.6	25.6	19.6	33.3
1959	108.0	47.3	25.3	17.1	30.9
1960	110.8	48.3	25.8	19.0	31.3
1961	111.2	46.1	28.7	17.3	31.9
1962	107.9	44.7	32.3	16.5	30.9
1963	128.8	59.7	34.7	20.1	37.8

Notes: 1. Monetary G.D.P. figures from 1946 to 1953 are obtained from unofficial estimates by H. W. Ord, "The Growth of Money Incomes in East Africa", *The East African Economics Review*, Vol. 9, No. 1 (June 1962). The later figures are from official sources and are, therefore, not strictly comparable with earlier years, though the difference is unlikely to be large.

2. Exports include exports to Kenya and Tanganyika, but exclude re-exports. The figures for 1959 and subsequent years exclude excise duty on excisable commodities and customs duty charged on imported raw materials used for local manufacture. In statistics for previous years the above duties were included in the valuation. The difference, however, is not likely to exceed £2m. or so for earlier years and is much less for later years. See also note (1), Table I.

3. "Government Expenditure" refers to the recurrent and non-recurrent expenditure of Central Government. After 1953, the financial year was changed from the calendar year to run from July to June. The figures for 1954 and subsequent years are the average of two financial years.

4. Includes imports from Kenya and Tanganyika as well as from countries outside East Africa; it excludes re-exports; see also note (1), Table I and note (2), Table II.

Sources: Annual Statistical Abstracts, 1955-63; *Background to the Budget 1965-66* (Ministry of Finance, May 1965).

II The Tax Structure

A detailed analysis of the Uganda fiscal system will be found in later chapters. Here it is intended merely to give a general over-all picture of the tax system and to discuss some of its major characteristics.

The Uganda tax system displays many of the features common to underdeveloped countries. Table III summarizes the revenues from major sources for both central and local governments.

It will be noticed from the table that the most characteristic feature of the Uganda fiscal system is its overwhelming dependence on taxes on foreign trade, mainly on imports and cotton and coffee exports. In 1963-64, Central Government derived over 66% of its total tax revenue from import and export duties. This, of course, is a reflection of the importance of foreign trade in the economy. While heavy reliance on import duties is a feature common to almost all developing countries, Uganda has also made skilful use of export duties to tax a large number of small scale farmers.

Another important feature of the Uganda tax system is the relatively small amount of revenue derived from the taxation

TABLE III (a)
The Tax Structure in Uganda
Central Government 1963/64

Tax Source				£m.	%
Income tax	..	..	..	3.74	14.6
Export taxes	..	..	..	7.87	30.8
Import duties	..	..	..	9.00	35.3
Excise duties	..	..	..	3.81	14.9
Licences etc.	..	..	..	1.11	4.3
				25.53	100.0

Source: Uganda Government: Financial Statement and Revenue Estimates 1965/66.

TABLE III (b)
Local Government, Estimates 1964/65

Tax source				£m.	%
Personal taxes	..	..	..	4.2	80.8
Property taxes		..	..	0.4	7.7
Other	..	..	..	0.6	11.5
Total	..	..	..	5.2	100.0

Source: J. F. Due, "Reform of East African Taxation", *The East African Economic Review* Vol. 11, No. 2 (December, 1964.)

of consumption of domestically produced goods and services. The main instrument for taxing these is the excise taxes, which bring in roughly 15% of the total tax revenue. Services are hardly taxed, while beer, sugar, cigarettes and tobacco are the only considerable revenue earners among the domestically produced goods.

Thirdly, revenue from income tax, as in many other developing countries, forms a relatively small proportion of Central Government revenue. This again is a reflection of the small importance of the corporate sector in the economy as well as of relatively generous personal allowances. In 1961, only 9,600 persons or 0.14% of the total population contributed to individual income tax revenue, while about 1,264 companies were assessed for company taxation. An overwhelming proportion of those taxed were non-Africans.

Table III(b) shows that well over 80% of the local governments' tax revenue is derived from graduated personal taxes. The latter are a kind of local income tax, adapted to the circumstances in East Africa. They are levied on income, actual or presumed, from all sources, including land and other assets used for subsistence. A widespread use of this tax establishes the principle of direct taxation for virtually all persons[7].

The other sources of local government tax revenue are property tax in urban areas, court fees, fines and trading and other licences. But their overall importance is relatively small.

The fiscal system is affected in several ways by Uganda's participation in the East African Common Market and related services[8]. The existence of the common market necessitates a high degree of fiscal co-ordination among the three East African countries; as a result, most major taxes such as company and individual income tax, customs and excise duties, are uniform throughout East Africa. This uniformity is desirable if the common market is to work smoothly and efficiently, but it introduces an element of rigidity into the system and further reduces the ability of the governments to manipulate fiscal policy to aid the task of development. Up till now, East African countries have been faced with broadly similar fiscal problems and hence it has been easier to secure agreement on revision

7. For a discussion of this and other features of the Uganda system, see J. F. Due: "Reform of East African Taxation", *op. cit.* Graduated Personal taxes are discussed in detail in *Report of Uganda Fiscal Commission*, Uganda Government (Entebbe: Government Printer, 1962), para. 42-53; see also U.K. Hicks, *Development from Below* (Oxford: The Clarendon Press, 1961) pp. 292-294.

8. For a detailed discussion of the fiscal implications of economic integration in East Africa, see J. F. Due and P. Robson, "Tax Harmonization in the East African Common Market", in *Tax Harmonization in Common Markets* edited by C. Shoup (Columbia University Press, forthcoming).

of rates on different taxes. But it is highly likely that in future with differing rates of economic growth and size of development plans and a more vigorous use of fiscal policy, the fiscal constraint imposed by the Common Market will be felt more acutely and generate greater friction. The last two to three years have already seen some divergence in the common fiscal pattern in the three countries; the indications are that this trend will be intensified in future.

The major taxes mentioned above are assessed, levied and collected by the East African Common Services Organization on behalf of the three East African Governments; this joint administration of common taxes undoubtedly results in substantial economies and is an excellent example of the benefits to be derived from inter-country co-operation in the provision of skilled and highly technical services in underdeveloped countries.

Since 1961, there has also been a measure of fiscal compensation to Uganda and Tanganyika to offset the unequal territorial distribution of benefits flowing from the existence of the Common Market[9]. According to the scheme, 40% of the proceeds of income tax charged to companies on profits arising from manufacturing and finance, and 6% of the annual revenue collected in the three countries from customs and excise duties are paid into a 'distributable pool'. One-half of the total receipts of the pool are distributed to the East African Common Services Organization to finance its non-self-contained services, while the other half are shared in equal parts among the three countries. This results in a redistribution of revenue from Kenya to Uganda and Tanganyika to the tune of about £½ million or so.

III Conclusion

The economy as well as the fiscal system of Uganda reveal characteristic features of an underdeveloped country. Some attempt has been made to adapt the tax system to local economic conditions e.g. in the general use of Graduated Personal Tax and heavy reliance on export taxes. Apart from income tax, the administrative costs involved in the assessment and collection of taxes are comparatively low. While no systematic thought has been given to the use of fiscal policy to force the pace of development, the tax system does embody some provisions designed to encourage savings and investment. Reliance on export taxes has enabled the government, especially during boom years, to raise a substantial amount of revenue in taxes.

---

9. See *East Africa: Report of the Economic and Fiscal Commission.*

One of the weaknesses of the present tax structure as will be shown in the subsequent chapters, is that it is unlikely to be sufficiently income elastic in the coming years to provide the required revenue to finance rising public expenditure.

Another serious defect of the current tax system is its regressive nature. While no systematic study has been carried out on the distribution of the tax burden in Uganda, there are indications to show that low-income rural dwellers, especially growers of cotton and coffee, pay a substantially higher proportion of their income in taxes than the middle-income and upper-income urban dwellers. There is some evidence to show that amongst urban dwellers, independent professional workers and businessmen come off relatively better than salaried persons because of the ease with which the former can escape their due tax liability[10]. There might be a case for regressive tax structure if it could be shown that this contributed significantly to economic growth in Uganda. But it is highly doubtful whether the existing distribution of tax burden in Uganda has been designed to accelerate the rate of economic growth. On the other hand, there are strong indications that high personal incomes in the non-agricultural sectors could be taxed more heavily with substantial benefit to public revenue but without any serious adverse effects on incentives[11].

---

10. The worst example of discriminatory tax legislation—the exemption of Africans from the payment of income tax—was abolished in 1961. See D. Walker, "Africans and Income Tax in Uganda", *The East African Economic Review* Vol. IV. (January, 1958) pp. 68-74.

11. For a detailed discussion of tax reform in East Africa, see J. F. Due, "Reform of East African Taxation", *op. cit.*, and D. P. Ghai, "Tax Structure for Rapid Economic Growth in East Africa" in *Problems of Economic Development in East Africa* (East African Publishing House, 1965).

Chapter III

GROWTH AND CHANGES IN THE COMPOSITION OF CENTRAL GOVERNMENT TAX REVENUE: 1948-63

I Introduction

The purpose of this chapter is to analyze the expansion of Central Government tax revenue in Uganda in the post-war period. It is hoped that this analysis will yield some insights into the main characteristics of the tax system, including its responsiveness to changes in income. Ideally we should have attempted to measure the income elasticity of the tax system as a whole as well as of its individual components. But an exercise of this nature is virtually made impossible by the lack of information necessary to eliminate the revenue effects of a large number of tax changes which took place during this period. Instead, it was decided to estimate the 'buoyancy' of various taxes, which would relate tax revenues to monetary G.D.P. over the period covered, but without making any allowance for the revenue effects of changes in tax rates and tax bases. The results of this calculation are discussed in the Appendix to this chapter.

The main body of the chapter is devoted to a detailed study of the growth and changes in the structure of central government tax revenue in the period 1948-63. The general method employed is to study over time changes in the ratio of the revenues from five important taxes to monetary G.D.P., and to attempt to explain these changes in terms of changes in tax rates and the relative importance of tax bases.

II Growth in Tax Revenue

Table I shows the growth of Central Government tax revenue in the post-war period. Perhaps the most remarkable feature of the fiscal system during this period is a phenomenally rapid growth of tax revenue between 1948 and 1952—very nearly a three-fold increase in four years. This of course is a reflection of the extra-ordinarily rapid growth of the economy during these years, caused primarily by a boom in cotton and coffee prices. The period since 1952, on the other hand, has been characterized by a relatively slow growth in tax revenue; this is especially true of the period

mention as footnote

1957-62 when tax proceeds were virtually stagnant[1]. This again is a reflection of stagnation in monetary G.D.P. between 1957 and 1962, caused in the main by a substantial and sustained fall in export prices of cotton and coffee.[2] Tax proceeds showed a sharp rise in 1963 owing to a large increase in monetary G.D.P., caused both by larger export crops and improved export prices.

Tax revenue fell sharply in 1953 mainly because of the collapse in commodity prices consequent upon the cessation of the Korean War; it also fell in 1960 and 1961 due to reduced export earnings which in turn were the result of lower crops due to adverse weather conditions.

It is perhaps more illuminating to study the changes in the ratio of tax revenue to monetary G.D.P. (T/Y); this ratio may also be used as a rough index of "the burden of taxation" on the economy. It must be remembered, however, that this measure ignores the fiscal burden imposed by the operations of the marketing boards, which was quite considerable in the immediate post-war years. Table III(a) shows that over the period as a whole, T/Y has remained fairly constant at around 15-16 per cent. Furthermore, there is no distinct trend upwards or downwards. There are certain years—1953, 1960 and 1961—when T/Y fell sharply and others—1963—when it rose sharply. But a detailed examination of these ratios does not bring out any systematic correlation between fluctuations in Y and T/Y. However even if such a correlation existed, this would not provide any evidence on the degree of the responsiveness of the tax system, as there were several changes in tax rates, tax bases etc. during this period. The only conclusion that may be drawn from these aggregate ratios is that the tax effort made by the country has not increased over the period.

We can, however, refine our index of tax burden in two ways. In the first place, we should compare total tax payments (central government as well as local authorities) with Y, and not merely central government tax proceeds. This is done in Table III(b). It will be noticed that the ratio of total tax to Y between 1957 and 1961 averages out to 18.3 per cent; but the period is too short for us to draw any conclusions regarding the trend in the burden of taxation.

---

1. The sharp increase in tax revenue in 1962, shown in Table I, in fact took place in 1963. It is shown in 1962 because of our method of calculating tax revenue for calendar year by averaging revenue in two financial years.
2. See Table II, chapter II.

TABLE I
Growth of Central Government tax revenue in Uganda 1948-63
£'000

	1948	1949	1950	1951	1952	1953	1954[1]	1955	1956	1957	1958	1959	1960	1961	1962	1963[2]
Income tax	400	602	661	639	1,169	1,785	2,189	2,756	3,160	3,078	3,231	3,533	3,542	3,567	3,670	3,805
Estate tax	20	12	36	9	38	7	27	40	37	43	71	55	41	29	29	38
Poll, Education tax etc.	721	513	537	571	605	629	863	528	553	599	628	619	606	570	343	376
Total direct tax	1,141	1,127	1,234	1,219	1,812	2,421	3,079	3,324	3,750	3,720	3,930	4,207	4,189	4,166	4,042	3,919
Export taxes	1,449	2,968	4,167	8,106	8,269	4,045	6,626	5,808	6,166	6,256	5,662	4,985	3,302	2,175	2,543	5,837
(Coffee export tax)	339	295	1,158	2,107	1,776	1,405	2,632	2,576	2,567	3,073	3,283	2,465	1,074	472	1,070	3,870
(Cotton export tax)	1,106	2,668	2,977	5,907	6,442	2,601	3,936	3,144	3,574	3,193	2,399	2,477	2,177	1,649	1,430	1,930
Import duties	1,565	1,761	2,080	2,888	2,995	3,308	3,776	4,260	4,222	4,128	4,643	5,340	5,914	6,307	7,706	9,019
Excise taxes	489	663	635	973	923	997	1,426	1,629	2,055	2,525	2,473	2,285	2,423	2,675	2,959	3,442
Licences etc.	180	199	228	239	261	336	419	416	418	480	613	709	647	654	897	947
Total Indirect taxes	3,685	5,591	7,110	12,206	12,448	8,686	12,747	12,113	12,861	13,387	13,391	13,319	12,286	11,811	14,105	19,245
Total Tax Revenue	4,824	6,718	8,344	13,425	14,260	11,107	15,326	15,437	16,611	17,107	17,321	17,526	16,475	15,977	18,147	26,164

Notes: 1. From 1954 the financial year runs from July to June; therefore total revenue as well as individual tax revenues for 1954 and later years are obtained by averaging two financial years.
2. 1963 figures are revised estimates.

Source: Annual Statistical abstracts 1955-64 Uganda: the figures for 1963 are derived from "Financial Statement and Revenue Estimates 1964/65" Uganda Government.

TABLE II

Percentages of various taxes in total Tax Revenue

Item	1948	1949	1950	1951	1952	1953	1954	1955	1956	1957	1958	1959	1960	1961	1962	1963
Income tax ..	8.3	9.0	7.9	4.8	8.2	16.1	14.3	17.8	19.0	18.0	18.7	20.2	21.5	22.3	20.2	16.4
Estate Duty	0.4	0.2	0.5	0.07	0.3	0.06	0.2	0.3	0.2	0.2	0.4	0.3	0.2	0.2	0.2	0.1
Poll, Education tax etc.	14.9	7.6	6.4	4.2	4.2	5.7	5.6	3.4	3.3	3.5	3.6	3.5	3.7	3.6	1.9	0.3
Total direct tax ..	23.6	16.8	14.8	9.07	12.7	21.86	20.1	21.5	22.5	21.7	22.7	24.0	25.4	26.1	22.3	16.9
Export taxes	30.0	44.2	50.0	60.4	58.0	36.4	43.2	37.6	37.1	36.6	32.7	28.4	20.0	13.6	14.0	25.2
(Coffee Export tax)	7.0	4.4	13.9	15.7	12.5	12.6	17.2	16.7	15.5	18.0	19.0	14.1	6.5	3.0	5.9	16.7
(Cotton Export tax)	22.9	39.7	35.7	44.0	45.2	23.4	25.7	20.4	21.5	18.6	13.9	14.1	13.2	10.3	7.9	8.3
Import Duties ..	32.5	26.2	24.9	21.5	21.0	29.8	24.6	27.6	25.4	24.1	26.8	30.5	35.9	39.5	42.5	38.9
Excise taxes ..	10.2	9.9	7.6	7.3	6.5	9.0	9.3	10.6	12.4	14.7	14.3	13.0	14.7	16.7	16.3	14.9
Licences etc.	3.7	3.0	2.7	1.8	1.8	3.0	2.7	2.7	2.5	2.8	3.5	4.1	3.9	4.1	4.9	4.1
Total Indirect Tax ..	76.4	83.3	85.2	90.95	87.3	78.2	79.8	78.5	77.4	78.2	77.3	76.0	74.5	73.9	77.7	83.1

TABLE III (a)

Tax revenues as percentages of monetary gross domestic product

ITEM	1948	1949	1950	1951	1952	1953	1954	1955	1956	1957	1958	1959	1960	1961	1962	1963
Monetary Gross Domestic Product £m. (Y)	30.3	42.8	54.3	83.8	88.3	76.3	92.8	102.0	102.8	109.4	106.0	108.0	110.8	112.1	107.9	128.7
Total tax revenue	15.92	15.69	15.37	16.02	16.15	14.56	16.51	15.13	16.16	15.64	16.34	16.23	14.87	14.25	16.82	17.80
Export tax (T_E)	4.79	6.94	7.68	9.68	9.37	5.31	6.21	5.70	6.00	5.72	5.34	4.62	2.98	1.94	2.35	4.54
Coffee Export Tax (T_{E_F})	1.12	0.70	2.14	2.52	2.02	1.85	2.46	2.53	2.50	2.81	3.09	2.29	0.97	0.42	0.99	3.01
Cotton Export Tax (T_{E_C})	3.66	6.24	5.49	7.05	7.29	3.41	3.69	3.08	3.47	2.91	2.26	2.30	1.97	1.47	1.33	1.50
Import Tax (T_M)	5.12	4.11	3.81	3.44	3.39	4.33	3.37	4.68	3.73	3.97	4.42	4.82	5.25	5.64	6.65	7.18
Excise Tax (T_x)	1.62	1.54	1.18	1.16	1.02	1.34	1.24	1.66	2.09	2.19	2.41	2.12	2.09	2.42	2.68	2.89
Individual Income Tax (T_p)	n.a.	n.a.	0.64	1.11	1.23	1.70	1.37	1.49	1.34	1.26	1.44	1.58	1.71	1.75	1.84	n.a.
Corporate Tax (Tc)	n.a.	n.a.	0.70	0.79	0.85	0.88	0.95	1.07	1.14	1.53	1.23	1.32	1.13	1.22	1.68	n.a.

Sources: (1) Monetary G.D.P. figures from 1948 to 1953 are derived from H. W. Ord, "The Growth of Money Incomes in East Africa", *The East African Economic Review*, Vol. 9, No. I (June 1962) pp. 41–47; the figures for subsequent years are obtained from "*The Real Growth of the Economy of Uganda, 1954–62*", Uganda Government, and "*Background to the Budget, 1964–65.*"

(2) Import tax and excise tax revenue are derived from *Annual Trade Reports*, East African High Commission (1948–61) and East African Common Services Organization (1962–63). They are slightly different from the figures used in Table I because they relate to calendar and not to financial year.

(3) Individual income tax and company tax figures are derived from the *Annual Income Tax Department Reports*, 1950–62, and are shown in Tables VII and VIII. They differ from the figures for income tax shown in Table I because they relate to the income of the year against which they are shown, whereas figures based on the Government budget relate to an earlier year, since income tax in Uganda is collected a year in arrears.

(4) Export tax figures are the same as in Table I. It will be noticed that total export tax yield is slightly less than the sum of cotton and coffee tax revenue, owing to the inclusion of an export tax on hides and skins.

It might be argued that an even better measure of the tax burden is the comparison of T/Y with income per head[3]. Table IV presents this comparison over the period 1948-1963.

It will be noticed from the above table that per capita monetary income after rising very rapidly from 1948 to 1951, has remained substantially unchanged in the subsequent period; while the ratio of tax revenue to monetary income has fluctuated between 14 to 17 per cent, with perhaps a very gradual trend upwards. More specifically, we might conclude that the burden of taxation in relation to income was relatively high in the years 1948-52 and was relatively light in the years 1955-57 and 1960-61. However, as income per capita has remained practically unchanged between 1951 and 1962, it is difficult to say whether the tax system a as whole has been "progressive" i.e. a larger proportion is paid in taxes as income rises[4].

III Changes in the Structure of Tax Revenue

Table II shows the changes in the relative importance of different taxes in the post-war period. The most characteristic feature of the Uganda fiscal system is its overwhelming dependence on taxes on foreign trade, which have brought in well over 60 per cent of total tax revenue every year except for 1961-62; in 1951-52 their contribution to revenue was as high as 80 per cent. However, within this total, the relative importance of export and import taxes has undergone considerable changes. Export taxes,

TABLE III (b)
Central and Local Government Tax Revenue: 1957—1961
£ '000

	1957	1958	1959	1960	1961
Local Government:					
Direct taxation	2,606	2,810	2,840	2,873	2,801
Indirect taxation	184	200	245	277	288
TOTAL	2,792	3,010	3,085	3,150	3,089
Central Government tax	17,107	17,321	17,526	16,475	15,977
GRAND TOTAL	19,899	20,331	20,611	19,625	19,066
Monetary G.D.P. ..	109,375	105,931	107,982	110,815	112,068
Total Tax/Y ..	18.19	19.19	19.09	17.71	17.01

Source: Annual Statistical Abstracts, Uganda Government.

3. Unfortunately this refers only to Central Government taxes; comparable figures for local government are not available prior to 1957.
4. The exclusion of subsistence income from our base gives a downward bias to T/Y. The process of economic growth is accompanied by a rise in the share of monetary income in total national income and since taxes are paid from monetary income, the process of monetization has a buoyancy effect on the ratio of tax to total income. I am indebted to Dr. R. H. Green for this point.

TABLE IV
Burden of Taxation

Year			Monetary income per head £	Tax Revenue Monetary G.D.P.
1948	..	..	6.13	15.92
1949	..	..	8.52	15.69
1950	..	..	10.64	15.37
1951	..	..	16.17	16.02
1952	..	..	16.90	16.15
1953	..	..	14.28	14.56
1954	..	..	16.14	16.51
1955	..	..	17.30	15.13
1956	..	..	17.00	16.16
1957	..	..	17.65	15.64
1958	..	..	16.68	16.34
1959	..	..	16.58	16.23
1960	..	..	16.59	14.87
1961	..	..	16.38	14.25
1962	..	..	15.38	16.82
1963	..	..	17.90	17.80

Source: Population figures are derived from Annual Statistical Abstract; for G.D.P. and tax-figures, see Tables I and III.

almost wholly on cotton and coffee, have played a dominant role in the Uganda tax system; they increased dramatically between 1948 and 1952, raising their relative importance from 30 per cent to about 60 per cent. However, the subsequent period saw a steady decline both in their absolute and relative importance until in 1961-62 they accounted for less than 14 per cent of total tax revenue. This trend was reversed in 1963 when there was a sharp rise in proceeds from export taxes. Within the category of export taxes, cotton export tax has steadily fallen in importance since 1952, while coffee export tax has shown a relative increase: in 1951-52, revenue from cotton was about 3½ times the revenue from coffee, whereas in 1963 it was only half the revenue from coffee.

The obverse of a secular decline in the relative importance of export taxes is, of course, an increase in the relative importance of other main taxes such as income tax, import and excise taxes. All these taxes have shown a strong upward trend and have, to some extent, offset the instability in tax revenue introduced by the volatility of proceeds from export taxes. Import tax revenue which accounted for about 28 per cent of total revenue in 1948-50, had risen to over 40 per cent in 1961-63. Since 1959 it has replaced the export tax as the single most important source of revenue to the Central Government. Likewise both excise taxes and income tax (including both individual and corporate tax) have shown a steady increase both in relative and absolute terms between 1951-52 and 1961-62. It is only in 1963 with a sharp rise in export tax revenue that all the other taxes have declined in relative importance.

These changes in revenue from individual tax sources have partly been influenced by changes in tax rates and/or tax bases. Thus the growth of a particular tax revenue is no indication of its income elasticity. In order to understand better the factors influencing the yield from various taxes, it is essential to separate out the revenue effects of changes in tax rates and tax bases. This has been attempted in the following section.

IV Analysis of Changes in the Yield of Some Important Taxes

In this section it is intended to analyse the changes in the yield of the five most important taxes with respect to changes in Y. The detailed analysis of each individual tax will throw further light on the structural changes in the fiscal system outlined in the last section. The general method employed is to seek an explanation of changes in the ratio of tax revenue to Y through an analysis of changes in rates of taxation and in the relative importance of the tax base in national income. This method should make explicit all the variables affecting yield from different taxes and perhaps enable us to formulate tentative conclusions about the income elasticity of these taxes.

(1) *Export Taxes*

Our approach to an analysis of export taxes can conveniently be summarised in the following four equations[5].

$$(a) \quad \frac{TE}{Y} = \frac{TE_c}{Y} + \frac{TE_F}{Y}$$

$$(b) \quad \frac{TE}{Y} = \left(\frac{E_c}{Y} \cdot \frac{TE_c}{E_c} \right) + \left(\frac{E_F}{Y} \cdot \frac{TE_F}{E_F} \right)$$

$$(c) \quad TE_c = f(R, P, V)$$

$$(d) \quad TE_F = f(R, P, V)$$

The first two equations break export taxes into their coffee and cotton components, while the last two spell out the main determinants of the yield from both these taxes i.e. price of cotton or coffee, quantity exported and the tax rate schedule.

The data corresponding to the first two equations are presented in Tables V, VI(*a*) and (*b*). A careful study of these tables brings out several interesting features of the behaviour of export taxes in the post-war period. Firstly, we notice that export taxes as

---

5. For the meaning of various symbols, see "Key to Notation" p. 31.

TABLE V

Export taxes, cotton and coffee exports and monetary G.D.P.

Item	1948	1949	1950	1951	1952	1953	1954	1955	1956	1957	1958	1959	1960	1961	1962	1963
Monetary G.D.P. (£m.) (Y)	30.3	42.8	54.3	83.8	88.3	76.3	92.8	102.0	102.8	109.4	106.0	108.0	110.8	112.1	107.9	128.7
Cotton and Coffee Exports (E) £'000	10,705	20,234	25,030	42,351	42,288	28,336	34,355	36,520	35,006	39,063	38,968	34,116	31,917	30,695	28,500	41,500
Export taxes (T_E)	1,449	2,968	4,167	8,106	8,269	4,045	6,626	5,808	6,166	6,256	5,662	4,985	3,302	2,175	2,500	5,800
E/Y	35.33	47.27	46.09	50.53	47.79	37.14	37.02	35.80	34.05	35.70	36.76	31.59	28.81	27.38	26.41	32.25
T_E/E	13.50	14.64	16.52	18.92	19.43	14.14	19.29	15.66	17.54	16.04	14.58	14.49	10.19	6.91	8.77	13.98
T_E/Y	4.79	6.94	7.68	9.68	9.37	5.31	6.21	5.70	6.00	5.72	5.34	4.62	2.98	1.94	2.35	4.54

Key to Notation		
Monetary Gross Domestic Product	=	Y
Total tax revenue of Central Government	=	T
Revenue from export taxes	=	T_E
Revenue from Cotton export taxes	=	T_{E_C}
Revenue from Coffee export taxes	=	T_{E_F}
Revenue from import duties	=	T_M
Revenue from excise duties	=	T_X
Revenue from Corporate taxes	=	T_C
Revenue from individual income tax	=	T_p
Revenue from licences	=	T_L
Revenue from all other taxes	=	T_o
Cotton and Coffee exports	=	E
Cotton exports	=	E_c
Coffee exports	=	E_F
Retained imports	=	M
Composition of imports	=	G
Value of excisable goods consumed	=	X
Profits	=	O
Undistributed profits of corporate bodies	=	Y_c
Taxable income of employees and individuals	=	Y_p
Tax rate schedule	=	R
Price level	=	P
Volume	=	V
Allowances	=	A
Pattern of income distribution by income groups	=	Y_D
Proportion of residents' to non-residents' income	=	Y_s

a proportion of monetary G.D.P. (T_E/Y) rose sharply between 1948 and 1952, increasing from 4.8 per cent to 9.4 per cent; but the general trend in the post-1952 period, with the exception of a few years such as 1954, 1956 and 1963, has been a decline in T_E/Y, with especially marked falls in 1953 and 1960-62. The years 1950 to 1952 must be treated as abnormal; ignoring these years then, we find that the trend in the value of T_E/Y has been a gradual decline, becoming especially marked in the 1959-62 period. We further find that in 8 out of 15 years changes in T_E/Y were in the same direction as changes in both the average rate of taxation (T_E/E) and in the relative importance of exports in monetary income (E/Y). But where the two diverge, it is the tax rate which in all cases except for 1952, determines the direction of the change in T_E/Y, mainly because of the greater proportionate change in it from year to year.

The second important fact that emerges from a study of the Tables VI(a) and (b) is that, ignoring the years 1950-52 as abnormal, cotton export tax revenue as a proportion of monetary income (TE_c/Y) shows a downward trend almost throughout the period; the decline in T_E/Y in the period 1954-58 would, therefore, have been greater but for an upward trend in the ratio of coffee export tax revenue to monetary income (TE_F/Y); the latter, however, reinforced the downward trend in TE_c/Y in the years 1959-61. We further observe that the decline in $^TE_c/Y$, ignoring once again the period 1950-52, was largely due to a downward trend in E_c/Y i.e. the share of cotton exports in monetary income; the average rate of taxation (TE_c/E_c) declined substantially only in the period 1958-61. With regard to coffee, the gradual upward trend in TE_F/Y throughout the period except for 1960-61, was largely the result of an increase in E_F/Y i.e. the share of coffee exports in monetary income. The fall in E_F/Y in some years e.g. 1954 and 1956, was offset by a sharp increase in the average rate of taxation (TE_F/E_F). The latter showed an upward trend until 1954 but has tended to decline in the subsequent period; it rose again in 1963.

Finally, it is worth remarking that for every year except 1954, 1958 and 1963, the average rate of duty on cotton has been substantially higher than the duty on coffee.

The next step in our analysis is to attempt an explanation of the trends in the behaviour of export taxes noted above[6]. As far as coffee and cotton export earnings are concerned, the general picture is clear enough: a very rapid expansion from 1948 to 1952 was followed by a virtual stagnation between 1954 and 1962. This period, however, witnessed a gradual increase in the relative importance of coffee exports at the expense of cotton exports. The most remarkable development here is an almost seven-fold increase in the volume of Robusta coffee exports between 1949 and 1963, most of the increase taking place in three sharp jumps in 1955, 1960 and 1963. Export earnings, however, did not rise proportionately, owing to a steady and substantial deterioration of coffee prices between 1954-61, as shown in Table VII. In contrast to coffee, the quantity of cotton exported has shown no distinct upward trend during this period; it was less in 1963 than in 1949-50. This, coupled with a downward trend in export prices since 1952,

6. This section relies heavily on Y. Kyesimira's paper entitled "Comparison of Agricultural Export Achievements in the East African Countries", *Economic Development Research Project* Paper No. 47: (East African Institute of Social Research, Kampala, 1964) mimeo.

TABLE VI (a)

Cotton exports, cotton export tax and monetary G.D.P.

ITEM	1948	1949	1950	1951	1952	1953	1954	1955	1956	1957	1958	1959	1960	1961	1962	1963
Cotton Exports (E_c)	7,458	17,343	16,698	28,697	29,943	16,793	20,877	16,386	19,285	17,476	18,141	15,428	14,930	16,716	8,300	14,300
Cotton Export tax (T_{E_c}) ..	1,106	2,668	2,977	5,907	6,442	2,601	3,936	3,144	3,574	3,193	2,399	2,477	2,177	1,649	1,430	1,930
E_c/Y	24.61	40.52	30.75	34.24	33.91	22.01	22.50	16.06	18.76	15.97	17.11	14.29	13.47	14.91	7.69	11.11
T_{E_c}/E_c ..	14.83	15.38	17.83	20.58	21.51	15.49	18.85	19.19	18.53	18.27	13.22	16.05	14.58	9.86	17.23	13.50
T_{E_c}/Y ..	3.66	6.24	5.49	7.05	7.29	3.41	3.69	3.08	3.47	2.91	2.26	2.30	1.97	1.47	1.33	1.50

TABLE VI (b)

Coffee export tax, coffee exports and monetary G.D.P.

£'000

Item	1948	1949	1950	1951	1952	1953	1954	1955	1956	1957	1958	1959	1960	1961	1962	1963
Coffee Export tax (T_{E_F})	339	295	1,158	2,107	1,776	1,405	2,632	2,576	2,567	3,073	3,283	2,465	1,074	472	1,070	3,870
Coffee Exports (E_F) ..	3,247	2,891	8,332	13,654	12,345	11,543	13,478	20,134	15,721	21,587	20,827	18,688	16,987	13,979	20,200	27,200
E_F/Y	10.72	6.75	15.34	16.29	13.98	15.13	14.52	19.74	15.29	19.73	19.65	17.30	15.33	12.47	18.72	21.13
T_{E_F}/E_F ..	10.44	10.20	13.9	15.43	14.39	12.17	19.53	12.79	16.33	14.23	15.76	13.19	6.32	3.38	5.30	14.23
T_{E_F}/Y ..	1.12	0.70	2.14	2.52	2.02	1.85	2.46	2.53	2.50	2.81	3.09	2.29	0.97	0.42	0.99	3.01

as shown in Table VII, accounts for the sluggishness in cotton export earnings in the last decade.

While export earnings are a function of the price and volume of exports, the rate of export taxation in Uganda depends solely on the price of exports. As far as cotton (A. R. Quality) is concerned there is a price floor below which no duty is levied; beyond that level, the average rate of taxation rises with price increases, tending towards a constant marginal rate of 24 per cent. This, however, was changed in April, 1961 and the marginal rate fell to 20 per cent. Thus under the present rates, the maximum average rate cannot exceed 20 per cent, though it could and did exceed this figure prior to 1961. There has been no other change in cotton export tax rate schedule during this period. We may, therefore, conclude that until 1961, the changes in average tax rate on cotton can be explained exclusively by reference to cotton export prices; this is borne out by comparing the changes in T_{Ec}/E_c with the cotton export price index shown in Table VII[7].

TABLE VII
Quantity and Price Indices of Cotton and Coffee Exports
1960-62 = 100

Year		Robusta Coffee		Arabica Coffee		Cotton	
		Quantity Index	Price Index	Quantity Index	Price Index	Quantity Index	Price Index
1949	..	21	87	10	68	136	96
1950	..	26	184	28	143	121	105
1951	..	36	225	47	141	120	179
1952	..	34	229	23	129	132	171
1953	..	30	234	26	151	117	108
1954	..	32	245	42	181	137	114
1955	..	61	191	77	151	107	115
1956	..	51	175	56	174	131	110
1957	..	72	181	60	167	125	105
1958	..	68	191	57	134	135	101
1959	..	75	150	79	113	130	89
1960	..	101	100	85	105	115	97
1961	..	88	93	80	101	122	103
1962	..	111	106	135	96	63	99
1963	..	142	120	110	86	115	94

Source: Y. Kyesimira, *op. cit.*, derived from Table IV(*b*): Uganda Agricultural Exports: 1949-63.

---

7. However, two sources of discrepancy accounting for divergence in direction between the changes in T_{Ec}/E_c and export prices may be noted: firstly, export prices shown here are obtained by dividing annual cotton export earnings by the quantity exported; but this average may, and usually does, conceal considerable monthly or even weekly or daily price fluctuations. Because of the nature of the export tax rate schedule, it is possible for T_{Ec}/E_c to rise even though the average price as defined here falls. Secondly, while export figures are collected on a calendar year basis, export tax revenue figures are available only on a financial year basis. Revenue figures for a calendar year have been derived by averaging two financial years. This clearly is the explanation for a sharp fall in T_{Ec}/E_c in 1961 and an equally sharp rise in 1962: the value of cotton exports in 1962 was half that in 1961, while tax revenue during these two years is partly influenced by export earnings in the preceding and following years.

To what extent have changes in T_{EF}/E_F been the result of changes in tax rate schedule rather than in coffee export prices? Strictly speaking, we should break coffee export earnings and tax revenue into its robusta and arabica components; but since the former provides an overwhelming proportion of coffee exports, we need concern ourselves only with robusta prices and tax rates. Up to August, 1956, the price floor for robusta below which no duty was levied was £36 per ton; beyond this floor there was a constant marginal rate of taxation of 20 per cent. In August, 1956, the floor was raised to £90 per ton f.o.b., and the marginal rate to $28\frac{4}{7}$ per cent; at the then ruling prices, this change had the effect of raising the average rate of taxation in 1956. The price floor was again raised to £120 per ton in June, 1957 and the marginal rate to $33\frac{1}{3}$ per cent. This had the effect of lowering the average rate of taxation in 1957; and this effect was intensified in subsequent years because of the fall in the price of coffee. The price floor was restored to its 1956 level of £90 per ton in April, 1963, but the marginal rate was kept at its higher level of $33\frac{1}{3}$ per cent.

We, therefore, see that from 1948 to 1955, T_{EF}/E_F was determined by export price movements; in 1956, T_{EF}/E_F would have fallen in sympathy with the fall in coffee export prices but for the change in rate schedule which raised the average rate of taxation at the then ruling prices; in 1957 exactly the opposite happened—although export prices rose, the average tax rate fell, due mainly to another change in the tax rate schedule, which had the effect of lowering the average tax rate at the then ruling prices. From 1958 to 1962 there was no change in the rate schedule and T_{EF}/E_F moved in the same direction as export prices; however, in 1963 the change in the rate schedule reinforced the effect of rising prices to raise T_{EF}/E_F above what it would have been otherwise. Thus we notice that unlike cotton, the average rate of tax on coffee has been influenced significantly by changes in rate schedules in addition, of course, to price changes.

2. (*Import Duties*)

Once again our approach to an analysis of changes in import tax revenue can best be summarised in the following equations:

$$\frac{T_M}{Y} = \frac{M}{Y} \cdot \frac{T_M}{M}$$

$$T_M = f(V, P, R, G)$$

The first equation shows that the yield of import duties with respect to income can be studied in two parts: the proportion of imports to monetary income and the average rate of import taxation. The data corresponding to this equation are presented in Table VIII. The second equation shows the determinants of revenue from import duties.

Next to export taxes, import duties have been the most important source of tax revenue to the Central Government in Uganda in the post-war period. Since 1959 they have been the single most important tax source. Our interest, however, is in the yield from import duties relative to monetary income. Table VIII shows that T_M/Y declined between 1948 and 1952, but has shown a strong upward trend since 1956, rising from 3.73 per cent in 1956 to 7.18 per cent in 1963. We further observe that the downward trend in T_M/Y from 1948 to 1952 was caused jointly by T_M/M and M/Y; the former declining every year except 1951, with the latter falling sharply in 1951.[8] What is of greater interest is to note that M/Y has shown a general downward trend since 1953; therefore, the upward trend in T_M/Y noted earlier, has been solely due to a rapid increase in the average rate of import taxation from 1955 onwards. The contrast with export taxes is illuminating: there has been a relative contraction in imports, as in exports, but unlike export taxes, the yield from import duties relative to monetary income has risen in recent years. The reason for this, as already indicated, is that, unlike export taxes, the average rate of import taxes has shown an upward trend.

We must now attempt to provide an interpretation of the above trends. The import bill in any given year is a function of the level of monetary income and more importantly of gross capital formation. The latter rose sharply in the early post-war period until 1955, but has shown a downward trend in the subsequent period. It will be noticed that this pattern is closely paralleled by retained imports, which have tended to decline after reaching a peak of £33.6m. in 1955. Gross capital formation has tended to decline after an investment boom between 1950 and 1955, because of the slowing down in the expansion of the economy, levelling off of export earnings, and more recently because of the uncertainties caused by the transformation of Uganda from a colonial to an independent country.

Turning now to the average rate of import taxation, changes in T_M/M could come about either as a result of changes

8. Throughout this study, unless otherwise stated, imports are meant to refer to imports from outside East Africa. We exclude imports from Kenya and Tanganyika from our base as they enter Uganda duty-free. However, rising inter-territorial imports have kept the ratio of total imports to monetary G.D.P. just about constant during this period.

TABLE VIII
Import duties, retained imports and monetary G.D.P.
£'000

Item	1948	1949	1950	1951	1952	1953	1954	1955	1956	1957	1958	1959	1960	1961	1962	1963
Import duties (Tm)	1,550	1,760	2,070	2,880	2,990	3,300	3,600	4,770	3,830	4,340	4,680	5,210	5,820	6,320	7,180	9,240
Retained Imports (M)	9,386	12,781	16,392	21,892	23,814	25,431	24,745	33,572	27,016	27,894	26,023	24,397	24,692	24,485	22,900	27,900
M/Y	30.98	29.86	30.19	26.12	26.97	33.33	26.66	32.91	26.28	25.50	24.55	22.59	22.29	21.84	21.22	21.68
Tm/m	16.51	13.78	12.63	13.16	12.56	12.98	14.55	14.21	14.18	15.56	17.98	21.36	23.57	25.81	31.35	33.12
Tm/Y	5.12	4.11	3.81	3.44	3.39	4.33	3.88	4.68	3.73	3.97	4.42	4.82	5.25	5.64	6.65	7.18

Notes;   1. Retained imports refer to total imports minus re-exports; they, however, exclude imports from Kenya and Tanganyika.

Source;   Annual Statistical Abstracts; Annual Trade Reports of Kenya, Uganda and Tanganyika: 1948-63.

in import duty rates or in the composition of imports. It is important to separate out these effects as they have a close bearing on the income elasticity of import duties. It is not possible to go into the details of all the changes in the import duty rates during this period. The general tendency, however, is clear. From 1948 to 1953, there was a general reduction in import duties from the high level reached during the War. Since 1955, the general tendency seems to have been towards an increase in import duties, except for 1957. This tendency has been especially marked since 1958. But we do not have adequate information to work out quantitatively the revenue effects of changes in import duties.

It thus appears that changes in $^TM/M$ can be adequately accounted for by changes in import duty rates. Have there been any changes in the composition of imports during this period and if so, what effect have they had on $^TM/M$? Tables IX(*a*) and (*b*) present comprehensive data on imports and yield from import duties broken down by categories for the period 1949-53 and 1954-63 respectively[9].

Tables IX(*a*) and (*b*) show the wide divergence of average import duty rates on different categories of imports. Turning first to the 1949-53 period, it will be noticed from Table IX(*a*) that four categories of imports—textiles; food, drink and tobacco; machinery, apparatus, vehicles etc; and products for heating, lighting, power etc. (mostly fuel)—have provided most of the import tax revenue. It is especially noteworthy that food, drink and tobacco, accounting for a mere 2 to 5 per cent of retained imports, contributed on an average slightly less than one fifth of the total yield from import taxes during the period; this, of course, is a reflection of a very high rate of import duties imposed on these goods. Textiles are another important category of imports: during this period, they accounted for slightly less than 25 per cent of retained imports and 30 per cent of import tax yield, though their relative importance in both these respects fell sharply in 1952 and 1953. The later years of this period witnessed the beginning of an investment boom which is partly reflected in the increasing relative importance of the "machinery, apparatus, appliances, vehicles" category. Lastly, products for heating, lighting lubricants etc. (mostly fuel), accounting for 5-6 per

---

9. S.I.T. classification is available only from 1954; the data for earlier years are classified on a different basis, and hence are not strictly comparable with subsequent years. Furthermore, the 1949-53 figures relate to retained imports, while 1954 and subsequent figures refer to "net home consumption" i.e. net imports minus government imports. Since there is no duty on the latter, net home consumption would appear to be a better base. However, it includes re-exports; import duty is not refunded on all re-exports.

TABLE IX (a

Import duty revenue and structure of foreign imports

1949

Category	Value of Imports	% of total Imports	Import Duty	% of total Import Duty	Average Duty %
1. Food, drinks and tobacco	498,818	3.89	243,008	13.82	48.72
2. Chemicals and allied products	369,503	2.88	8,293	2.75	13.07
3. Rubber	292,671	2.28	45,405	2.58	15.51
4. Paper	300,108	2.34	17,825	1.01	5.94
5. Textiles	3,499,432	27.30	649,731	36.94	18.57
6. Articles of clothing—all materials	567,311	4.43	53,474	3.04	9.43
7. Products for heating, lighting, power etc.	658,728	5.14	238,600	13.57	36.22
8. Non-metallic minerals and manufacture thereof	581,297	4.54	41,325	2.35	7.11
9. Base metals and Manufacture thereof	1,714,254	13.37	111,758	6.35	6.52
10. Machinery, apparatus, appliances and vehicles	3,474,239	27.10	203,483	11.57	5.86
11. Other	861,272	6.72	105,855	6.02	12.29
TOTAL	12,817,633		1,758,757		

1950

Category	Value of Imports	% of total Imports	Import Duty	% of total Import Duty	Average Duty %
1. Food, drinks and tobacco	742,952	4.82	278,175	13.41	37.44
2. Chemicals and allied products	362,586	2.35	45,236	2.18	12.48
3. Rubber	386,026	2.51	56,639	2.73	14.67
4. Paper	343,792	2.23	20,590	0.99	5.99
5. Textiles	3,971,322	25.78	755,015	36.41	19.01
6. Articles of clothing—all materials	931,291	6.05	76,142	3.67	8.18
7. Products for heating, lighting, power etc.	830,827	5.39	267,503	12.90	32.20
8. Non-metallic minerals and manufacture thereof	664,993	4.32	48,696	2.35	7.32
9. Base metals and Manufacture thereof	2,189,101	14.21	135,997	6.56	6.21
10. Machinery, apparatus, appliances and vehicles	4,218,880	27.39	237,128	11.43	5.62
11. Other	760,356	4.9	152,677	7.4	20.1
TOTAL	15,402,126		2,073,798		

1951

Category	Value of Imports	% of total Imports	Import Duty	% of total Import Duty	Average Duty %
1. Food, drinks and tobacco	1,177,583	5.32	507,863	17.64	43.13
2. Chemicals and allied products	619,408	2.80	70,715	2.46	11.42
3. Rubber	784,261	3.54	76,727	2.67	9.78
4. Paper	652,583	2.95	56,177	1.95	8.61
5. Textiles	5,923,655	26.76	928,967	32.27	15.68
6. Articles of clothing—all materials	1,510,586	6.82	75,129	2.61	4.97
7. Products for heating, lighting, power etc.	1,028,958	4.65	275,635	9.58	26.79
8. Non-metallic minerals and manufacture thereof	1,218,098	5.50	74,390	2.58	6.11
9. Base metals and Manufacture thereof	3,057,885	13.81	217,855	7.57	7.12
10. Machinery, apparatus, appliances and vehicles	5,118,583	23.12	382,135	13.28	7.47
11. Other	1,046,042	4.7	212,781	7.4	20.30
TOTAL	22,137,944		2,878,374		

1952

Category	Value of Imports	% of total Imports	Import Duty	% of total Import Duty	Average Duty %
1. Food, drinks and tobacco	614,310	2.53	457,853	15.31	74.53
2. Chemicals and allied products	808,271	3.33	78,693	2.63	9.74
3. Rubber	627,504	2.58	54,714	1.83	8.72
4. Paper	926,650	3.81	46,823	1.57	5.05
5. Textiles	5,264,410	21.67	874,808	29.25	16.62
6. Articles of clothing—all materials	877,704	3.61	57,670	1.93	6.57
7. Products for heating, lighting, power etc.	1,321,482	5.44	302,474	10.11	22.89
8. Non-metallic minerals and manufacture thereof	1,334,123	5.49	67,543	2.26	5.06
9. Base metal and manufacture thereof	3,330,968	13.71	214,396	7.17	6.44
10. Machinery, apparatus, appliances and vehicles	7,381,098	30.38	559,753	18.72	7.58
11. Other	1,809,718	7.40	276,128	9.2	15.3
GRAND TOTAL	24,296,238		2,990,855		

1953

Category	Value of Imports	% of total Imports	Import Duty	% of total Import Duty	Average Duty %
1. Food, drinks and tobacco	1,006,610	3.92	651,309	19.74	64.70
2. Chemicals and allied products	739,271	2.88	76,175	2.31	10.30
3. Rubber	706,700	2.75	78,867	2.39	11.16
4. Paper	376,510	1.47	18,465	0.56	4.90
5. Textiles	4,066,279	15.83	725,274	21.98	17.84
6. Articles of clothing—all materials	946,199	3.68	58,218	1.76	6.15
7. Products for heating, lighting, power etc.	1,761,670	6.86	338,687	10.26	19.23
8. Non-metallic minerals and manufacture thereof	1,440,227	5.61	72,713	2.20	5.05
9. Base metal and manufacture thereof	4,028,691	15.68	272,787	8.27	6.77
10. Machinery, apparatus, appliances and vehicles	7,689,727	29.93	517,833	15.69	6.73
11. Other	2,926,655	11.39	489,354	14.83	16.72
GRAND TOTAL	25,688,539		3,299,682		

Source: Statistical Abstract, 1955, Uganda.

TABLE IX (b)

Import duty revenue and structure of foreign imports
(net home consumption): 1954-63

Items	1954					1955				
	Imports £	% of total Imports	Import Duty £	Average Duty Rate	% of Total Duty	Imports £	% of total Imports	Import Duty £	Average Duty Rate	% of total Duty
1. Food .. .. .. :	1,277,634	5.4	112,092	8.8	3.1	1,397,568	4.3	146,306	10.5	3.1
2. Beverages and tobacco .. :	340,892	1.4	694,344	203.7	19.3	429,742	1.3	797,975	185.7	16.7
3. Crude Minerals, Inedible except Fuel .. .. :	82,554	0.4	2,921	3.5	0.08	102,493	0.3	7,606	7.4	0.2
4. Mineral Fuels, lubricants and related materials ..	1,619,252	6.9	379,472	23.4	10.5	1,909,298	5.9	497,291	26.0	10.4
5. Animal and Vegetable Oils, Fats .. : : :	93,732	0.4	585	0.6	0.02	107,000	0.3	1,730	1.6	0.04
6. Chemicals .. : :	761,060	3.2	82,760	10.9	2.3	1,139,138	3.5	121,318	10.6	2.5
7. Manf. goods classified chiefly by material .. :	9,438,422	39.9	1,206,113	12.8	33.5	12,014,699	37.3	1,500,786	12.5	31.5
8. Machinery & Transport equipment .. :	5,670,296	24.0	433,289	7.6	12.0	9,998,678	31.1	770,760	7.7	16.2
9. Misc. Manufac. articles	1,546,555	6.5	214,070	13.8	5.9	1,986,383	6.2	364,381	18.3	7.6
10. Misc. transactions and commodities n.e.s. ..	2,806,474	11.9	474,814	16.9	13.2	3,090,049	9.6	560,937	18.2	11.8
GRAND TOTAL ..	23,636,871		3,600,460	15.2		32,175,048		4,769,090	14.8	

TABLE IX (b)—(Continued)
Import duty revenue and structure of foreign imports
(net home consumption): 1954-63

Items	1956					1957				
	Imports £	% of Total Imports	Import Duty £	Average Duty Rate	% of Total Duty	Imports £	% of Total Imports	Import Duty £	Average Duty Rate	% of Total Duty
1. Food	970,691	3.7	124,445	12.8	3.3	935,942	3.5	118,595	12.7	2.7
2. Beverages and tobacco	214,666	0.8	536,371	249.9	14.0	195,998	0.7	688,599	351.3	15.9
3. Crude Minerals, Inedible except fuel	129,434	0.5	9,631	7.4	0.3	91,126	0.3	3,362	3.7	0.07
4. Mineral Fuels, lubricants and related materials	1,974,379	7.4	530,232	26.9	13.9	2,201,134	8.1	498,381	22.6	11.5
5. Animal and vegetable oils, fats	114,224	0.4	1,877	1.6	0.05	278,115	1.0	2,143	0.8	0.05
6. Chemicals	1,188,007	4.5	123,906	10.4	3.2	1,406,646	5.2	146,625	10.4	3.4
7. Manf. goods classified chiefly by material	10,025,108	37.8	1,307,181	13.0	34.2	11,103,176	41.0	1,566,088	14.1	36.1
8. Machinery and transport equipment	8,587,015	32.4	550,480	6.4	14.4	7,238,667	26.8	528,636	7.3	12.2
9. Misc. Manufac. articles	1,649,103	6.2	324,959	19.7	8.5	2,034,774	7.5	457,515	22.5	10.5
10. Misc. transactions and commodities n.e.s.	1,656,410	6.2	315,949	19.1	8.2	1,571,751	5.8	330,883	21.1	7.6
GRAND TOTAL	26,509,037		3,825,025	14.4		27,057,329		4,340,827	16.0	

TABLE IX (b)—(Continued)
Import duty revenue and structure of foreign imports (net home consumption): 1954-63

Items	1958 Imports £	% of Total Imports	Import Duty £	Average Duty Rate	% of Total Duty	1959 Imports £	% of Total Imports	Import Duty £	Average Duty Rate	% of Total Duty
1. Food	1,091,252	4.4	119,417	10.9	2.6	1,069,516	4.5	159,429	14.9	3.1
2. Beverages and tobacco	204,419	0.8	601,449	294.2	12.9	204,735	0.9	559,293	273.2	10.7
3. Crude Minerals, Inedibles except Fuel	210,823	0.8	2,654	1.3	0.06	90,311	0.4	1,755	1.9	0.03
4. Mineral Fuels, lubricants and related materials	2,234,994	8.9	657,737	29.4	14.1	2,111,645	8.9	728,080	34.5	14.0
5. Animal and vegetable oils, fats	240,149	1.0	2,432	1.0	0.05	278,452	1.2	2,833	1.0	14.0
6. Chemicals	1,478,375	5.9	132,971	9.0	2.8	1,621,616	6.8	123,135	7.6	2.4
7. Manf. goods classified chiefly by material	9,310,738	37.3	1,835,235	19.7	39.2	8,845,200	37.1	2,223,947	25.1	42.7
8. Machinery and transport equipment	6,838,217	27.4	491,677	7.2	10.5	6,490,841	27.2	584,541	9.0	11.2
9. Misc. transactions and commodities n.e.s.	1,313,045	5.3	327,033	24.9	7.0	1,129,350	4.7	301,791	26.7	11.2
10. Misc. Manufac. articles	2,052,955	8.2	505,134	24.6	10.8	1,984,515	8.3	525,263	26.5	10.0
GRAND TOTAL	24,974,967		4,675,739	18.7		23,825,181		5,210,067	21.9	

TABLE IX (b)—(continued)

Import duty revenue and structure of foreign imports
(net home consumption): 1954-63

	1960					1961				
Items	Imports £	% of Total Imports	Import Duty £	Average Duty Rate	% of Total Duty	Imports £	% of Total Imports	Import Duty £	Average Duty Rate	% of Total Duty
1. Food	1,846,069	3.5	160,040	18.9	2.8	928,709	3.8	178,007	19.2	2.8
2. Beverages and tobacco	198,620	0.8	532,380	268.0	9.1	214,309	0.9	551,314	257.3	8.7
3. Crude Minerals, Inedible except Fuel	116,523	0.5	2,136	1.8	0.04	182,663	0.8	2,050	1.1	0.03
4. Mineral Fuels, Lubricants and related materials	2,112,982	8.6	1,265,250	59.9	21.7	2,065,194	8.5	1,356,180	65.7	21.5
5. Animal and Vegetable Oils, Fats	651,343	2.7	6,764	1.0	0.1	368,071	1.5	8,431	2.3	0.1
6. Chemicals	1,659,760	6.8	120,125	7.2	2.06	1,825,722	7.5	165,351	9.1	2.6
7. Manf. goods classified chiefly by material	8,948,590	36.5	2,123,034	23.7	36.5	9,228,454	38.0	2,376,046	25.7	37.6
8. Machinery and Transport equipment	6,898,727	28.1	730,762	10.6	12.6	6,258,416	25.7	586,183	9.4	9.3
9. Misc. Manufac. articles	1,988,668	8.1	548,185	27.6	9.4	2,199,773	9.1	692,776	31.5	11.0
10. Misc. transactions and commodities	1,101,864	4.5	332,801	30.2	5.7	1,034,008	4.3	404,056	39.1	6.4
GRAND TOTAL	24,523,146		5,821,477	23.7		24,305,319		6,320,400	26.0	

TABLE IX (b)—(Continued)

Import duty revenue and structure of foreign imports

(net home consumption): 1954-63

Items	1962					1963				
	Imports £	% of Total Imports	Import Duty £	Average Duty Rate	% of Total Duty	Imports £	% of Total Imports	Import Duty £	Average Duty Rate	% of Total Duty
1. Food	1,134,828	4.7	201,872	17.8	2.8	1,011,974	3.5	204,883	20.2	2.2
2. Beverages and tobacco	193,807	0.8	501,542	258.8	7.0	199,008	0.7	510,083	256.3	5.5
3. Crude Minerals, Inedibles except Fuel	387,895	1.6	2,681	0.7	0.04	315,020	1.1	2,126	0.7	0.02
4. Mineral Fuels Lubricants and related materials	2,192,482	9.1	2,078,434	94.8	28.96	2,306,695	8.1	2,702,273	117.1	29.27
5. Animal and vegetable oils, fats	324,774	1.4	11,690	3.6	0.2	301,836	1.1	12,595	4.2	0.1
6. Chemicals	1,851,300	7.7	158,185	8.5	2.2	1,935,361	6.8	208,477	10.8	2.3
7. Manf. goods classified chiefly by material	8,186,694	34.1	2,436,424	29.8	83.9	9,978,052	35.0	3,002,466	30.1	32.51
8. Machinery and transport equipment	6,440,318	26.8	682,350	10.6	9.5	8,504,627	29.8	1,184,208	13.9	12.8
9. Misc. Manufac. articles	2,173,939	9.1	651,478	30.0	9.1	2,724,146	9.6	856,267	31.4	9.3
10. Misc. Transactions and commodities	1,134,475	4.7	452,164	39.9	6.3	1,237,682	4.3	549,747	44.4	6.0
GRAND TOTAL	24,020,512		7,176,820	29.9		28,514,401		9,233,125	32.4	

Source: Annual Trade Reports of Kenya, Uganda and Tanganyika 1954-63.

cent of retained imports, contributed well over 10 per cent of the yield from import duties.

A study of the 1954-63 period, the data for which are presented in Table IX(*b*), reveals a number of interesting facts. The structure of import duties in Uganda is designed to tax relatively heavily consumer goods, especially luxuries, and to tax lightly or even to admit duty-free most of the intermediate and investment goods. Table IX(*b*) shows that over the period as a whole there has been an upward trend in import duty rates, which has been especially marked since 1957: mineral fuels etc (S.I.T.C.4) show the most rapid increase in average import duty rate—a five-fold rise between 1954 and 1963; food (1), manufactured goods classified chiefly by material (7), and miscellaneous manufactured goods (9) experience a two-and-a-half-fold increase in import duty rates, while machinery and transport equipment (8) show a two-fold rise over the period 1954-63. It is only crude materials (3) and chemicals (6) which from 1957 to 1960 show a downward trend in the average rate of import duties.

Turning now to the composition of imports, we find that the relative importance of food (1), beverages and tobacco (2), and manufactured goods classified chiefly by material (7) has tended to decline over the period—an evidence of a successful policy of import substitution.[10] It will be noticed that all these categories, especially manufactured goods etc. (7), have been very important sources of tax revenue[11]. The relative contribution of manufactured goods classified chiefly by material (7) to import tax yield has, however, not fallen because of the progressive increase in tax rates. But the share of both food and beverages and tobacco has fallen, the latter from 19.3 per cent in 1954 to 5.5 per cent in 1963. This illustrates the type of fiscal problem that will become increasingly important in future as ambitious programmes of import substitution are launched and successfully carried through. Another category—chemicals—has doubled its share of net home consumption of imports; its contribution to import tax revenue has, however, remained small because of the low rate of duty levied on chemicals. This, again, illustrates another aspect of the fiscal problem arising from a change in the composition of imports that is bound to become more important in future. As might be expected the imports of machinery and transport equipment show considerable annual

---

10. To some extent, the foreign imports have been replaced by imports from Kenya. Thus it is more a case of import substitution within East Africa as a whole rather than in Uganda alone.

11. By far the most important import in this respect is textiles.

fluctuations; their share in revenue does not show any distinct trend. Finally, the table shows that the buoyancy of import tax revenue during this period has been very largely due to a rapid rise in the yield from mineral fuels, lubricants etc. (4); its share in imports has remained fairly constant since 1957 but its contribution to revenue has increased nearly five-fold over the period 1954-63. In 1963 it accounted for just over 8 per cent of imports and nearly 30 per cent of import tax revenue.

We must, therefore, conclude that the increase in T_M/M since 1956 has been the result of increases in average rates of import duties by legislation rather than a consequence of greater consumption of relatively heavily taxed imports. In fact whatever changes in the composition of imports have taken place have been in the direction of reducing the average rate of import taxation.

3. Excise Duties

Our approach to the analysis of the yield from excise duties may be summarized in the following equations:

(a) $T_X = T_{beer} + T_{sug.} + T_{cig.} + T_{tob.}$

(b) $T_X = f(R_{beer}, V_{beer}) + f(R_{sug.}, V_{sug.}) + f(R_{cig.}, V_{cig.})$
$\qquad + f(R_{tob.}, V_{tob.})$

The first equation shows excise revenue as a function of revenue from the main excisable commodities; the second equation spells out the determinants of revenue from each of these commodities.

The share of excise duties in total tax revenue (T_X/T) declined between 1948 and 1952, from 10.2 per cent to 6.5 per cent, but it has shown an upward trend in the subsequent period. Likewise, Table III(a) shows that T_X/Y declined between 1948 and 1952, from 1.6 per cent to 1.0 per cent, but has risen steadily in the subsequent period, amounting to 2.9 per cent in 1963.

It is unfortunately not possible to analyze changes in T_X/Y in terms of changes in X/Y and T_X/X, as figures on the value, as opposed to the quantity, of excisable goods consumed are not available. Excise revenue in Uganda is obtained principally by duties on domestically produced beer, sugar, cigarettes and tobacco. The duties are levied on specific rather than *ad valorem* basis. It may be of interest to analyse the changes in the structure of excise tax revenue during this period. Tables X(a), (b) and (c) present comprehensive data on the revenue from principal excisable goods, quantity of excisable goods consumed, and changes in the rate of excise duties over the period 1948-63.

TABLE X (a)

Composition of excise revenue: Uganda 1948-63

Item	1948	1949	1950	1951	1952	1953	1954	1955	1956	1957	1958	1959	1960	1961	1962	1963
Beer £	14,484	16,691	31,126	53,312	109,526	120,472	148,821	275,004	336,063	395,275	451,590	337,094	378,623	549,408	627,266	742,776
Percentage of total Excise Revenue	3.0%	2.5%	4.9%	5.5%	12.2%	11.8%	11.2%	16.2%	15.6%	16.5%	17.7%	14.7%	16.3%	20.3%	21.7%	20.0%
Sugar: £	27,322	48,020	54,997	76,730	75,385	85,842	168,157	246,866	306,437	647,713	717,529	555,678	563,162	749,805	864,448	1,183,432
Percentage of total Excise Revenue	5.6%	7.3%	8.7%	7.9%	8.4%	8.4%	12.7%	14.6%	14.2%	27.0%	28.2%	24.3%	24.3%	27.6%	29.9%	31.8%
Cigarettes	284,725	393,089	344,167	656,669	527,800	606,318	792,104	909,547	1,195,602	1,080,918	1,123,599	1,151,374	1,156,589	1,181,346	1,202,585	1,545,541
Percentage of total Excise Revenue	58.2%	59.3%	54.2%	67.7%	58.8%	59.2%	59.9%	53.7%	55.7%	45.1%	44.1%	50.3%	49.8%	43.6%	41.6%	41.5%
Tobacco £	154,751	189,970	196,423	186,724	185,065	211,664	214,092	262,756	314,475	272,072	253,599	244,561	223,584	229,107	196,164	225,880
Percentage of total Excise Revenue	31.6%	28.7%	30.9%	19.2%	20.6%	20.6%	16.2%	15.5%	14.6%	11.4%	10.0%	10.7%	9.6%	8.4%	6.8%	6.1%
Others : £	7,754	14,733	8,340	2,686	556	—	—	89	22	87	—	—	40	2,074	3,149	23,524
Percentage of total Excise Revenue	1.6	2.2	1.3	—	—	—	—	—	—	—	—	—	—	0.1	0.1	0.6
Total Excise Revenue	489,036	662,503	635,053	970,949	897,220	1,024,296	1,323,174	1,694,262	2,152,577	2,396,065	2,546,295	2,288,707	2,321,998	2,711,740	2,893,612	3,720,653

Source: Annual Trade Reports of Kenya, Uganda and Tanganyika: 1948-63.

TABLE X (b)

Composition of main excisable commodities : 1948-63 : Uganda

Item	1948	1949	1950	1951	1952	1953	1954	1955	1956	1957	1958	1959	1960	1961	1962	1963
Beer Imperial gallon	126,119	139,006	296,102	442,799	601,139	827,371	935,376	1,668,813	2,063,947	2,370,264	2,806,000	1,772,824	1,948,464	2,787,786	2,774,668	2,828,841
Sugar: Cwt.	264,656	447,222	480,548	645,948	686,531	752,333	803,766	965,119	1,083,878	1,139,923	1,219,842	1,276,618	1,243,239	1,430,479	1,301,624	1,506,196
Cigarettes: lb.	736,551	1,010,955	970,981	1,641,910	1,424,404	1,722,987	1,856,648	1,960,730	1,940,660	1,977,784	2,010,447	2,082,077	2,065,573	2,164,090	1,985,048	2,308,739
Tobacco: lb.	460,683	521,533	553,234	558,290	606,489	618,862	602, 2	574,217	512,556	494,677	461,089	444,655	406,517	416,559	356,435	409,481

Source: Annual Trade Reports of Kenya, Uganda and Tanganyika: 1948-63.

TABLE X (c)

Duty per unit of main excisable commodities

| Item | 1948 | 1949 | 1950 | 1951 | 1952 | 1953 | 1954 | 1955 | 1956 | 1957 | 1958 | 1959 | 1960 | 1961 | 1962 | 1963 |
	Sh. cts	Sh. cts.	Sh. cts	Sh. cts.	Sh. cts.	Sh. cts.	Sh. cts.	Sh. cts.	Sh. cts.	Sh. cts.	Sh. cts.	Sh. cts.	Sh. cts.	Sh. cts.	Sh. cts.	Sh. cts.
Beer per Imperial Gallon	2.20	2.40	2.20	2.40	3.60	3.00	3.20	3.20	3.20	3.40	3.20	3.80	3.80	4.00	4.60	5.20
Sugar Per Cwt. .	2.07	2.15	2.37	2.38	2.19	2.28	4.18	5.12	5.65	11.36	11.76	8.71	9.06	10.48	13.28	15.71
Cigarettes per lb. ..	7.72	7.78	7.10	7.98	7.42	7.04	8.54	9.28	12.32	10.94	11.18	11.06	11.20	10.92	12.12	13.38
Tobacco per lb. ..	6.72	7.28	7.10	6.68	6.10	6.84	7.10	9.16	12.28	11.00	11.00	11.00	11.00	11.00	11.00	11.00

Source: Annual Trade Reports of Kenya, Uganda, Tanganyika : 1948-63.

Table X(a) shows that there have been significant shifts in the relative importance of revenue from different excisable goods: although cigarettes still continue to be the most important revenue earner, their relative importance has declined from over 57 per cent in 1948-50 to just over 41 per cent in 1962-63, most of the decline occurring after 1956. Likewise, the share of revenue from tobacco has shown a persistent decline; it fell from 30 per cent in 1948-50 to just over 6 per cent in 1962-63. On the other hand, the share of revenue from both beer and sugar recorded significant increases, the former rising over six-fold from 3.4 per cent in 1948-50 to 20.8 per cent in 1962-63, and the latter over four-fold from 7.2 per in 1948-50 to 30.8 per cent in 1962-63. The share of beer went up sharply in 1952 and 1955, while that of sugar increased dramatically in 1957 and to a lesser extent in 1954.

We must try to assess the relative importance of changes in tax rates and in the amount of exisable goods consumed in explaining the changes in the structure of excise revenue observed above. This information is contained in Tables X(b) and (c). One of the most notable features here is the behaviour of consumption of manufactured tobacco, which after increasing very rapidly between 1948 and 1952, has declined steadily since 1953, so that less tobacco was consumed in 1963 than in 1948. This is undoubtedly due to a progressive substitution of cigarettes for tobacco; it will be noticed that the consumption of domestically produced cigarettes has increased well over two-fold between 1948-50 and 1962-63. On the other hand, the excise rates on cigarettes and manufactured tobacco have gone up by just under 75 per cent and 65 per cent respectively between 1948 and 1963. Thus the sluggishness in revenue from tobacco is wholly due to a decline in the quantity of tobacco consumed over the period; the relative importance of revenue from cigarettes has declined because of the failure of both excise rates and cigarette consumption to rise at a sufficiently fast rate.

Tables X(b) and (c) show further that although the duty on beer has more than doubled between 1948-50 and 1962-63, by far the greater proportion of increase in beer revenue has been due to an increase in beer consumption which has risen by fifteen-fold over the same period. Of all the excisable commodities, sugar has suffered the greatest increase in tax rates, which went up $5\frac{1}{2}$ times between 1948-50 and 1962-63. However, most of this increase occurred in two sharp jumps in 1954 and 1957. Despite the sharp rise in excise duty rates, the consumption of sugar increased $3\frac{1}{2}$ times over the same period. We may summarize our discussion by saying that the share of revenue from sugar has increased due to a sharp rise in tax rates as well as a substantial increase in sugar consumption, while the share of revenue from beer has increased primarily due to a dramatic increase in beer consumption.

4. Individual Income Tax

Individual income tax is levied on employees as well as on one-man firms and partnerships. The behaviour of the yield of individual income is especially interesting as this is the only genuinely progressive tax in Uganda.

Our analysis of the yield from individual income tax will proceed along the lines summarized in the following equations:

$$(a) \quad \frac{T_p}{Y} = \frac{Y_p}{Y} \cdot \frac{T_p}{Y_p}$$

$$(b) \quad T_p = f(Y_p, R, A, Y_D, Y_S)$$

As usual, the first equation states that the individual income tax revenue as a proportion of monetary income (Y) can be looked upon as a product of the share of taxable income in Y and the average rate of taxation. The second equation spells out the principal determinants of income tax revenue—personal taxable income, tax rate schedule, allowances, pattern of income distribution and the proportion of residents' to non-residents' taxable income.

Information relating to the first equation is presented in Table XI(a). It will be noticed that despite falls in occasional years e.g. 1954, 1956-57, T_p/Y shows a distinct upward trend over the

TABLE XI (a)
Personal "Taxable" incomes, individual income tax, and monetary G.D.P. 1948-62
£'000

Year	Individual Income Tax[1] (Tp)	Personal Taxable Income (Yp)	Monetary G.D.P. £m. (Y)	Yp/Y	Tp/Yp	Tp/Y
1950	..	350	3,411	54.3	6.28	10.26	0.64
1951	..	930	6,768	83.8	8.08	13.74	1.11
1952	..	1,090	8,274	88.3	9.37	13.17	1.23
1953	..	1,300	10,247	76.3	13.43	12.69	1.70
1954	..	1,460	12,160	92.8	13.10	12.01	1.37
1955	..	1,520	13,509	102.0	13.24	11.25	1.49
1956	..	1,380	13,736	102.8	13.36	10.05	1.34
1957	..	1,380	14,429	109.4	13.19	9.56	1.26
1958	..	1,530	16,424	106.0	15.49	9.32	1.44
1959	..	1,710	17,440	108.0	16.15	9.81	1.58
1960	..	1,890	17,846	110.0	16.11	10.59	1.71
1961	..	1,960	17,804	112.1	15.88	11.01	1.75
1962	..	1,990	18,320	107.9	16.98	10.86	1.84

1. Personal taxable income is equal to aggregate income of "individuals" (one-man firms and partnerships) and employees minus interest paid and lossses suffered; it includes all personal allowances and deductions.
Source: East African Income Tax Department (Annual Reports, 1950-62).

period as a whole. Furthermore, the upward trend has been maintained in the face of a decline in T_p/Y_p from 1951 to 1958; it is

TABLE XI (b)

Taxable Income and Tax Assessed: Individuals and Employees
£'000

		INDIVIDUALS			*EMPLOYEES*		
Year		Taxable Income (a)	Tax assessed (b)	b/a	Taxable Income (c)	Tax assessed (d)	d/c
1950	..	1,038	146	14.07	2,373	201	8.47
1951	..	2,284	401	17.56	4,484	533	11.89
1952	..	2,609	449	17.21	5,666	644	11.37
1953	..	3,466	548	15.81	6,781	747	11.02
1954	..	3,917	561	14.32	8,243	900	10.92
1955	..	4,134	536	12.97	9,375	980	10.45
1956	..	3,800	444	11.68	9,936	931	9.37
1957	..	4,187	461	11.01	10,243	917	8.95
1958	..	4,831	522	10.81	11,594	1,007	8.69
1959	..	5,045	571	11.32	12,394	1,138	9.18
1960	..	5,118	662	12.93	12,728	1,230	9.66
1961	..	4,476	557	12.44	13,328	1,398	10.49
1962	..	4,059	473	11.65	14,261	1,518	10.64

Source: East African Income Tax Department (Annual Reports; 1950-62).

only from 1958 that T_p/Y_p has started rising. The main reason for the upward trend in T_p/Y is to be sought in the steady rise in Y_p/Y i.e. in the ratio of personal taxable income to total monetary income: between 1950 and 1962, Y_p/Y has risen $2\frac{1}{2}$ times from 6.3 per cent to 17 per cent.

Before we go on to interpret changes in Y_p/Y it is necessary to define the income tax base—Y_p. We are using Y_p for lack of any better index of personal income; it includes all the income (including gross dividends) of employees, partnerships and one-man firms assessed for income tax. The term covers both residents and non-residents. Until 1961 Africans were exempted from income tax. Moreover, as allowances and deductions have been fairly generous, only a tiny fraction of the working population is assessed for income tax. In 1961, a total of 12,400 individuals and employees were assessed. Lastly, as in other underdeveloped countries, it is very likely, owing to a fairly widespread practice of tax evasion and underdeclaration among businessmen, that Y_p is an underestimate of the income of the few people who are assessed.

Bearing these qualifications in mind, we can now proceed to a discussion of the changes in Y_p/Y noted above. The level of Y_p is determined by a number of complex factors such as the relative importance of unincorporated to total enterprises, the pattern of income distribution, the level of profits and allowances, dividend distribution policy, efficiency in coverage and assessment etc. We do not have enough information to assess quantitatively the relative importance of these factors. However, there are certain factors which have clearly favoured the rapid expansion of Y_p: these include the rapid growth of money incomes until the mid-fifties, resulting in a large increase in the number of persons with taxable incomes, improvements over time in coverage and assessment. There are reasons to believe that Y_p is rather flexible with respect to increases in Y but is inflexible when Y falls. A large proportion of Y_p consists of the income from employment and quarters of employees and individuals in upper income brackets, and as such it is unlikely to fall very much when Y falls due to a decline in export earnings. On the other hand, when there is a rise in Y, Y_p is likely to increase as well owing to a larger number of persons entering the taxable income category. Table XI(a) shows that Y_p/Y rose markedly in 1953 and 1958, the two years when there was a fall in Y; Y_p continued to show an increase despite a fall in Y. It is true that Y_p also includes an element of profits which are subject to considerable fluctuations in both directions, but they form a relatively small proportion of Y_p.

Personal allowances influence Y_p through their effect on the number of persons assessed for income tax. It will be shown below that during this period the only substantial increase in personal allowances was in 1957, which resulted in a fall in the number of assessments and also in the value of Y_p/Y for that year.

From our point of view it is of greater interest to interpret changes in the average rate of taxation (T_p/Y_p). As we have seen T_p/Y_p declined steadily between 1951 and 1958 and has shown an upward trend since then. Given Y_p, T_p is a function of allowances,

TABLE XII (a)
Chargeable Income as a Percentage of Actual Income 1950-62
£'000

Year		Actual Income[1] (a)	Chargeable Income[2] (b)	b/a
1950	.. ..	3,411	2,003	58.72
1951	.. ..	6,768	4,230	62.50
1952	.. ..	8,274	5,229	63.20
1953	.. ..	10,247	6,425	62.70
1954	.. ..	12,160	7,548	62.07
1955	.. ..	13,509	8,153	60.35
1956	.. ..	13,736	8,269	60.20
1957	.. ..	14,429	7,317	50.71
1958	.. ..	16,424	8,234	50.13
1959	.. ..	17,440	8,866	50.84
1960	.. ..	17,846	9,475	53.09
1961	.. ..	17,804	9,836	55.25
1962	.. ..	18,320	10,123	55.26

Notes: 1. "Actual income" is aggregate income less interest paid, losses, passage allowances, retirement benefit payments and alimony.
        2. "Chargeable income" is actual income less personal allowances.
Source: Annual Reports (1950-62), East African Income Tax Department.

rate schedule, distribution of income by income groups and by residence. The latter is important because allowances form a much smaller fraction of the income of non-residents who consequently bear a heavier rate of taxation.

Allowances clearly have an important influence on the average rate of taxation; Table XII(a) shows that throughout this period chargeable income i.e. total income minus allowances, has constituted only 50 to 60 per cent of the taxable income. Except for 1957 the changes in rates of personal allowances have been relatively unimportant: there was an increase in non-residents' allowances in 1953 and 1954; for residents there was some increase in 1952[12]. However, changes in non-residents' allowances are of small consequence, as they are not taken up in any case. The 1957 changes resulted in a very considerable increase in personal allowances for residents[13]. Table XII(a) shows that chargeable income (Personal taxable incomes minus deductions and allowances) as a proportion of total personal taxable income fell every year from 1952 to 1958, with a sharp fall in 1957, caused by an increase in personal allowances. The increasing relative importance of allowances and deductions is perhaps the most important reason explaining the fall in T_p/Y_p over this period. It is interesting to note that the decline in the relative importance of allowances since 1958 coincides with an upward trend in T_p/Y_p.

The next factor to consider is the rate schedule. There was only one change in tax rates—in 1957—during this period. The general effect was to raise rates of taxation for chargeable incomes

---

12. In 1952, the children's allowances for residents went up as follows:
First child from £80 to £120, the next three children from £40 to £60 per child. Education allowance from £50 to £75.
For non-residents the increase in allowances was as follows:

	Pre-1953 £	1953 £	1954 £
Single allowance	160	180	200
Marriage allowance	245	280	300
Children's allowance	60	85	85

These increases applied to non-residents in U.K.; there were similar increases for non-residents elsewhere.

13. *Pre-1957 rates*   *1957*
   (1) Single allowance—£200, which reduces by £1 for every £4 by which total income exceeds £200   £225 fixed.
   (2) Marriage allowances—£350   £500-700 depending on the income.
   (3) Children's allowance—£120 and £60 each for the next three children   Varies from £75 to £175 depending on age and education.
In 1961 there were some minor changes in allowances whose net effect was perhaps to reduce the relative importance of allowances. Marriage allowance was fixed at £700 instead of varying between £500 to £700. Children's allowances were to vary with their age. Education, dependents and old age allowances ≤ ere eliminated.

of up to £2000, and to lower slightly the rates on chargeable incomes in excess of £2,000. It is very difficult to determine whether the overall effect was to raise or to lower the average tax rate. Since about 75 per cent of chargeable income falls in the under £2,000 category, it is likely that the general effect was to raise slightly the over-all tax rate. This would have had the effect of moderating the fall in T_p/Y_p in 1957 and 1958, caused by a large increase in allowances. It is also worth remarking that the steepness of the rate schedule was increased considerably in 1957. This may be yet another reason for the upward trend in T_p/Y_p since 1958. In the earlier period the rate schedule was not sufficiently steep to offset the influence of increased allowances.

The proportion of non-residents' to total income is also relevant. Table XII(b) shows that allowances have tended to constitute only 2-3 per cent of actual income for non-residents, while they have been running at about 48 per cent for residents in recent years[14]; consequently the former bear an average rate of taxation (nearly 20 per cent) which is twice the average rate for residents[15]. We find that the proportion of non-residents' to total actual income declined every year between 1950 and 1957, from over 10 per cent to about 3.0 per cent; it has however, risen in the subsequent period. This is reflected even more clearly in Table XI (b), which breaks down the taxable income into its employees and individuals (partnerships, one-man firms) components. Most of the non-residents' income is classified under the category "individuals". The table shows that the decline in T_p/Y_p is largely, though not wholly, attributed to a decline in the average rate of taxation on the income of individuals, which in turn is primarily due to a fall in the share of non-residents' income. The changing importance of non-residents' income is, therefore, an additional important reason for the decline of T_p/Y_p from 1951 to 1957 and for its subsequent rise.

Finally, we must assess the revenue effects of changes in the distribution of income by income groups. We can best do this by isolating the influence of allowances i.e by considering the ratio tax assessed/chargeable income. This ratio fell between 1951 and 1956 and has shown an upward trend since then; the fall in this ratio is surprising in view of the progressive nature of the tax and of the fact that the average taxable income of resident

---

14. This presumably is due to the fact that non-residents claim personal allowances in their country of origin and are, therefore, not entitled to make similar claims in Uganda.

15. For a definition of actual income see notes to Table XII (b).

TABLE XII (b)

Residents' and non-residents' actual income,* allowances† and tax rates

	1950	1951	1952	1953	1954	1955	1956	1957	1958	1959	1960	1961	1962
1. Actual income of non-residents	343,607	485,197	562,560	541,193	569,210	472,447	406,567	432,017	594,151	617,086	636,187	777,470	530,358
2. Actual income of residents ..	3,057,972	6,267,867	7,691,970	9,677,372	11,559,385	12,979,673	13,272,874	13,932,801	15,674,403	16,483,774	16,882,283	16,706,419	17,460,181
3. Total actual income	3,401,579	6,753,064	8,254,530	10,218,565	12,128,595	13,452,120	13,679,441	14,364,818	16,268,554	17,100,860	17,518,470	17,483,889	17,990,539
4. (1) as % of (3)	10.1	7.2	6.8	5.3	4.7	3.5	3.0	3.0	3.7	3.6	3.6	4.4	3.0
5. Allowances for non-residents ..	9,927	7,515	7,600	10,201	10,489	9,896	15,746	11,238	15,929	8,144	n.a	34,943	40,835
6. (5) as % of (1)	2.9	1.5	1.4	1.9	1.8	2.1	3.9	2.6	2.7	1.3	—	4.5	7.7
7. Allowances for residents ..	1,388,620	2,525,100	3,018,419	3,783,119	4,570,319	5,289,399	5,394,911	7,037,007	8,018,519	8,226,655	8,043,765	7,613,049	7,827,094
8. (7) as % of (2)	45.1	40.3	39.2	39.1	39.5	40.8	40.6	50.5	51.2	49.9	47.6	45.6	44.8
9. Tax assessed for non-residents	67,900	111,208	145,728	131,264	130,853	85,993	60,476	78,703	109,492	120,189	129,260	145,490	59,204
10. (9) as % of (1)	19.76	22.92	25.90	24.25	22.99	18.20	14.87	18.22	18.43	19.48	20.32	18.7	11.2
11. Tax assessed for residents ..	300,716	823,367	947,481	1,164,047	1,330,658	1,429,902	1,314,837	1,339,661	1,466,715	1,637,898	1,814,382	1,864,838	1,989,984
12. (11) as % of (2)	9.83	13.14	12.32	12.03	11.51	11.02	9.91	9.62	9.36	9.94	10.75	11.2	11.4

Notes: *"Actual income" is defined as aggregate assessed income minus deductions for interest paid, losses, passage allowances, retirement benefit payments alimony and averaging.
†Allowances comprise single, married, children, life assurance allowances
Source: Annual Reports of the East African Income Tax Department: 1950-62.

tax-payers rose every year between 1950 and 1956 except for 1955. As there were no changes in the tax rate schedule during this period, the only explanation for the fall in the ratio tax assessed/chargeable income can be a more even distribution of chargeable income. Fortunately, the Income Tax Department Reports contain a fairly comprehensive picture of the distribution of chargeable income by income groups. These figures show that there has been a general tendency since 1951 towards a decline in the relative importance of higher incomes—of £2,000 and over, and to a lesser extent of the lowest incomes—up to £800, but a slight increase in the middle-incomes—£801-£1,999. We have seen that there was a change in the tax rate schedule in 1957, which resulted in a much steeper rate structure. Between 1958 and 1961, the ratio income tax assessed/chargeable income rose every year. This has been the result of an upward trend in average taxable income and a significant rise in the proportion of total chargeable income accruing to tax-payers with chargeable income of £1,600 and above. This would be an additional factor accounting for the upward trend in T_p/Y_p since 1958, while the tendency towards a slightly more even distribution of chargeable income between 1951 and 1956 contributed to the fall in T_p/Y_p during that period.

To summarize our analysis of the individual income tax, T_p/Y fell between 1951 and 1957 due to a decline in the average rate of taxation (T_p/Y_p) which in turn was the consequence of a relative increase in allowances, a decrease in the proportion of non-residents' to total actual income, and a more even distribution of chargeable income. T_p/Y has risen between 1957 and 1962, owing to a sharp increase in the tax base in 1958 but also due to a rise in the average rate of taxation, caused by a reversal of all the factors noted above.

5. Corporate Taxes

As with the other taxes, our approach to an analysis of corporate taxes may be summarised in the following equations:

$$(a) \quad \frac{T_C}{Y} = \frac{Y_C}{Y} \cdot \frac{T_C}{Y_C}$$

$$(b) \quad T_C = f(R, Y_C, 0)$$

Information relating to the first equation is presented in Table XIII. However, before we proceed to an analysis of changes in T_C/Y, it is necessary to say something about the structure of corporate taxes in Uganda[16]. Corporate tax is levied on companies, clubs and trusts. Furthermore, companies are divided into two categories: public and controlled companies. A company is "controlled" unless there is a public holding of more than 25 per cent of the voting power and of equity; if five persons or less hold or have held more than 60 per cent of the voting rights or of the equity, then there must have been dealings in 25 per cent of the shares; the "public" for this purpose excludes relations and nominees of other persons. Persons with 20 per cent or more of the voting power or equity are not part of the public: they are the potential controllers[17]. One-man firms and partnerships are treated as individuals and are not subject to corporate tax.

The taxation on controlled companies has been devised to ensure that as far as possible they are treated as partnerships. Until 1956, a company tax of Shs. 4 in the £ (20%) was levied on both the public and the "controlled" companies. But the Commissioner of Income Tax had powers to declare that a certain proportion of the income of "controlled companies" be deemed to have been

TABLE XIII
"Corporate chargeable income", corporate tax and monetary G.D.P. 1948-62
£'000

Years	Undistributed Profits[1] (Yc)	Corporate Tax[2] (Tc)	Monetary G.D.P. (Y)	Yc/Y	Tc/Yc	Tc/Y
1948	—	—	30.3	—	—	—
1949	—	—	42.8	—	—	—
1950	1,735	376	54.3	3.20	21.67	0.70
1951	3,013	658	83.8	3.60	21.84	0.79
1952	3,598	748	88.3	4.07	20.79	0.85
1953	3,190	668	76.3	4.18	20.94	0.88
1954	4,270	886	92.8	4.60	20.75	0.95
1955	5,443	1,086	102.0	5.34	19.95	1.07
1956	5,594	1,166	102.8	5.44	20.84	1.14
1957	5,800	1,667	109.4	5.30	28.74	1.53
1958	4,270	1,296	106.0	4.03	30.35	1.23
1959	4,647	1,431	108.0	4.30	30.79	1.32
1960	4,974	1,247	110.8	4.49	25.07	1.13
1961	4,331	1,367	112.1	3.86	31.56	1.22
1962	4,424	1,813	107.9	4.10	40.98	1.68

Notes: 1. "Undistributed profits" are arrived at after deducting all dividends paid from companies to individual persons as well as to other companies —from the aggregate corporate income. However, as dividends paid are usually from preceding year(s) income, this has the effect of over-estimating the undistributed profits in a period of rising dividends and conversely in a period of falling dividends.
2. Corporate tax on undistributed profits is similarly arrived at after deducting all tax paid at source on dividends.
Source: East African Income Tax Department: Annual Reports, 1950-62.

16. The analysis presented in this section traces the changes in corporate taxation until 1963. In 1965, there were further changes which are discussed in the next chapter.
17. *See Report of the Uganda Fiscal Commission*, para 77. (Government Printer, Entebbe, 1962.)

distributed and thus be liable to individual income tax. This procedure was adopted to prevent evasion of taxes by "controlled"
companies, as the company tax rate was considerably lower than
the individual income tax rate that would be levied if profits were
distributed to share-holders. In 1957, the tax rate on all corporate
bodies was raised to 5 shs. 50 cents in the £ ($27\frac{1}{2}\%$). The "controlled"
companies were in addition subject to an undistributed income tax
at the penal rate of 9 shs. 50 cents in the £ ($47\frac{1}{2}\%$), if they failed to
distribute a certain percentage of their profits as dividends. The
latter tended to vary with the type of business the company was
engaged in. Therefore, as far as "controlled" companies were
concerned, the basic tax rate was $27\frac{1}{2}$ per cent, which could rise
to 75 per cent if a certain percentage of profits were not distributed.
Distributed profits, on the other hand, are taxed at the effective
rate for the individual dividend recipients. Each individual receiver
is credited with the amount deducted at source. If his effective rate
exceeds the company rate, he pays the excess; if it falls short, he
can recover the difference. Similarly, undistributed profits of public
companies were taxed at $27\frac{1}{2}$ per cent, while distributed profits
suffered a tax rate appropriate to the individual income recipient.

In 1961 an additional corporation tax of 2 shs. in the £ (10%)
was levied on public companies. However, unlike the income tax of
5 shs. 50 cents in the £, the individual shareholder receives no credit
for the corporation tax. In 1962, the corporation tax was increased
to 3 shs. 50 cents in the £ while income tax on companies was reduced
from 5 shs. 50 cents to 4 shs. in the £ (20 %). In effect, therefore,
the profits made by public companies are taxed at a rate of 7 shs.
50 cents in the £ ($37\frac{1}{2}\%$), but the individual shareholders received
a credit of only 4 shs. in the £ (20%) on their dividends. The effective
rate on "controlled" companies was also raised to 7 shs. 50 cents
in the £ and the undistributed income tax reduced to 7 shs. 50 cents
in the £.

In our analysis of changes in corporate tax revenue, we shall
use undistributed profits as our tax base. Our reason for using
undistributed rather than the total profits is that distributed profits
have already been included in the incomes of individuals as dividends, and the tax assessed on them has also been attributed to
individuals. It would, therefore, be double-counting to include
distributed profits and the tax thereon in corporate income and
tax[18]. As shown in the notes to Table XIII, undistributed profits

---

18. However, since 1961 part of the company tax on distributed profits is
not creditable to shareholders; this part-corporation tax has been included in
corporate tax (see page 61).

and the tax levied on them have been obtained after considerable manipulation of the data contained in the Income Tax Department Reports. Even so, the tax base is not entirely satisfactory: in the first place the profit figures are exclusive of depreciation, investment allowances etc. granted to companies; it is, therefore, not possible to determine the revenue effects of any changes in these allowances. Secondly, and more importantly, undistributed profits are arrived at after deducting all dividends from the "actual income" of corporate bodies; the dividends given in any year are derived from the income of the preceding year(s). In a period of rising dividends, our method will, therefore, tend to over-estimate the amount of undistributed profits as the latter are given out of previous year's income and conversely when dividends are falling.

We can now proceed to an analysis of changes in T_c/Y over the period 1950-62. Table XIII shows that apart from two years, T_c/Y has shown a steady upward trend, rising from 0.70 per cent in 1950 to 1.7 per cent in 1962. This has been the result of an increase in both the share of undistributed profits in monetary income (Y_c/Y) and in the average rate of taxation (T_c/Y_c). The former rose steadily between 1950 and 1956, fell in 1957 and shows a mild upward trend since then. T_c/Y_c on the other hand, was reasonably stable between 1950 and 1956, rose sharply in 1957, fell in 1960 and has risen sharply since then.

We have seen that the corporate tax rate was 4 shs. in the £ (20%) until 1956[19]. T_c/Y_c rose in 1957 because of an increase in tax rate to 5 shs. 50 cents in the £ ($27\frac{1}{2}$%). The value of T_c/Y_c between 1957 and 1959 is, however, higher than $27\frac{1}{2}$ per cent; this may be a reflection of the penal rate of undistributed income tax imposed on some "controlled companies." The sharp decline in T_c/Y_c in 1960 is a complete mystery. The official statistics show that tax deducted at source amounted to over 40 per cent of the dividends received by companies; this figure should really be $27\frac{1}{2}$ per cent. The higher rate on dividends accounts for a lower tax rate on undistributed profits. There does not appear to be a satisfactory explanation for a 40 per cent rate on dividends. It is, therefore, difficult to escape the conclusion that there is an error in official statistics.

The rise in T_c/Y_c in 1961 is a reflection of an increase in the tax rate on public companies from 5 shs. 50 cents to 7 shs. 50 cents in the £ ($37\frac{1}{2}$%). That T_c/Y_c did not rise to $37\frac{1}{2}$ per cent is due

---

19. The minor deviations in Tc/Yc from 20 per cent are probably the result of statistical errors, as well as of small departures from the standard rate for certain kinds of businesses.

entirely to the considerable importance of "controlled companies" in Uganda, which continued to be taxed at the lower rate of 5 shs. 50 cents in the £. The sharp rise in T_c/Y_c in 1962 to 41 per cent is due to two reasons: the increase in tax rates on "controlled companies" from $27\frac{1}{2}$ per cent to $37\frac{1}{2}$ per cent and the fact that the corporation tax of 3 shs. 50 cents in the £ $(17\frac{1}{2}\%)$ is levied on total profits—distributed as well as retained—for which no deduction is allowed to dividend recipients.

Retained earnings of corporate bodies (Y_c) are a function of total business profits, the proportion of profits accruing to unincorporated enterprises, and of the proportion of retained to total profits in corporate enterprises. During periods of rapid expansion, we should expect Y_c to rise faster than Y; this probably is the most important reason for the increase in Y_c/Y between 1950 and 1956. Furthermore, the relatively lower rate of corporate taxation until 1956 must have provided a strong incentive to increase the proportion of undistributed to distributed profits by companies and for the conversion of one-man firms and partnerships into companies in order to avoid liability to individual income tax. Some support for the latter explanation comes from a study of the number of companies assessed for taxation which rose rapidly between 1949 and 1954. The fall in Y_c/Y in 1957 and 1958 can be explained by reference to the introduction of the penal undistributed income tax on "controlled" companies, which had the effect of discouraging the retention of profits. The relative stability of Y_c/Y between 1958 and 1962 can be explained by a stagnation of monetary income and increases in corporate tax rates, thereby stimulating distribution of profits and discouraging the conversion of unincorporated into incorporated enterprises.

To sum up our discussion of corporate taxes, T_c/Y has shown a fairly steady upward trend during the period 1950-62. This has been due to an increase in the relative importance of retained earnings by corporate enterprises from 1950 to 1956; in the subsequent period the increase in T_c/Y was entirely due to an increase in corporate tax rates.

IV Conclusion

It may be useful to summarize here the main conclusions derived from a study of the expansion of Central Government tax revenue in the post-war period. Over the period as a whole, the ratio of tax yield to monetary income has remained fairly constant. There have, however, been important changes in the relative importance of different taxes. The most important change has been the sustained fall in the yield of export taxes relative to monetary income in the post-1952 period. This has been caused mainly by a decline in the relative importance of cotton exports; the fall in T_E/Y would have been even greater but for the upward trend in the relative importance of coffee exports. All the other important taxes show an upward trend in the ratio tax yield/monetary income over the period as a whole, especially since 1958; though there are years when tax yield from particular taxes relative to monetary income fell a little. In general, the increase in the tax yield/monetary income ratio for import and excise duties was more the result of an increase in the average rate of taxation than in the ratio tax base/monetary income. However, for corporate taxes both these elements were important, though at different periods. Surprisingly, the progressive individual income tax stands out as one example of a tax which owed an increase in the ratio tax yield/monetary income primarily to an increase in its tax base relative to income, rather than to an increase in the average rate of taxation.

Finally, can we say anything about the income elasticity of the Uganda tax system and that of its component taxes? The elasticity of the entire tax system is strongly influenced by the responsiveness of export and import taxes because of their over-whelming importance in the Uganda tax system. Export taxes are highly income elastic if the main source of change in income is fluctuations in export prices. In the early post-war years, a sharp rise in export prices made export taxes and also the entire tax system, highly income elastic; whereas since 1954, a substantial and sustained fall in export prices has made export taxes inelastic, which has offset the buoyancy of some other taxes.

Imports are strongly influenced by export earnings. It would appear that import taxes would have been income inelastic because of the relative shrinkage of import base and a change in the composition of imports increasing the relative importance of products with relatively lower duty rates[20]. The fact that T_M/Y has shown an upward trend since 1954 has been due almost wholly to successive increases in import duty rates.

Excise tax revenue as a proportion of monetary income has shown an upward trend since 1952. We saw earlier that the greater proportion of increases in excise tax revenue was due to increases in tax rates. However, a study of Tables X(*a*), (*b*) and (*c*) shows that

---

20. While changes in import duty rates may have had some influence on the composition of imports, it is doubtful whether they had a significant effect on the total volume of imports.

even after deducting the increase in revenue due to increased tax rates, the excise tax still emerges as an income elastic tax[21]. If we further assume that the consumption of excisable goods would have risen faster if tax rates had been constant, the excise tax appears even more income elastic.

Turning now to income taxes, individual income tax has clearly been an income elastic tax due in the main to an increase in the tax base/monetary income ratio despite the granting of more generous personal allowances in 1957. Corporate tax, on the other hand, because of its proportionate rate structure, can be income elastic only if its base expands faster relative to monetary income. This seems to have been the case until 1956. In the subsequent period because of a stagnation in monetary income, the share of corporate income either remained constant or actually fell in a number of years.

We may, therefore, conclude that apart from the commodity boom period of 1948-52, which may be regarded as abnormal, export taxes have been income inelastic, as also have been import taxes. Excise taxes and individual income tax, on the other hand, have been income elastic. Lastly corporate tax has been elastic only in the earlier period of rapid expansion.

Excise and income taxes account for relatively small proportion of total tax revenue. It, therefore, appears that the tax system as a whole has been income inelastic because of the inelasticity of the two main taxes. The fact that the ratio of tax yield to monetary income has not fallen over the period is mainly due to successive increases in import, excise, corporate, and to a lesser extent, export tax rates at the end of the post-war boom.

---

21. Our calculations, based on Tables X(*a*), (*b*) and (*c*), show the following relative increases in the revenue, rates and quantities consumed of excisable commodities between 1952 and 1963:

	Revenue in 1963	*Quantities consumed 1963*	*Tax Rate in 1963*
	Revenue in 1952	*Quantities consumed 1952*	*Tax Rate in 1952*
Cigarettes	2.92	1.62	1.82
Beer	6.78	4.70	1.44
Sugar	15.70	2.18	7.17
Tobacco	1.22	0.68	1.84

Note: Comparable ratios for total excise tax revenue and monetary income for the period 1952-63 are 4.15 and 1.46 respectively.

APPENDIX I

Some Estimates of the 'Buoyancy' of Important Central Government Taxes in Uganda

It was mentioned earlier that owing to lack of data it did not prove possible to estimate the income elasticity of either the individual taxes or of the tax system as a whole. Instead it was decided to estimate the 'buoyancy' of various taxes, which would relate the changes in tax revenues to changes in monetary G.D.P. over the period covered but without making any allowance for changes in tax rates and tax bases. These estimates may also be considered as a measure of the tax effort made by the country.

For most of the taxes the period covered was 1948-63. It is realized that the estimates of monetary G.D.P. for the period 1948-53 are not based on as firm foundations as those for later years, but the advantage of obtaining a larger number of observations was felt to outweigh the disadvantage of using G.D.P. figures for earlier years. Furthermore, the period 1948-63 includes both years of rapid economic expansion and relative stagnation; while an analysis based on the period 1954-63 alone would have given us biased results.

Two types of equations were used to see which would give us a better fit. These equations were:

$$X = a+bY \qquad (1)$$
$$X = aY^b \qquad (2)\ (i)$$
$$\log X = \log a+b \log Y \qquad (2)\ (ii)$$

where X=tax revenue, Y=monetary G.D.P. and a and b are constants. The first equation is a simple linear regression equation and assumes constant marginal tax revenue/monetary G.D.P. ratio, while the second assumes a constant buoyancy ratio.

Our calculations showed that the buoyancy equation $(X=aY^b)$ gave a better fit. We shall, therefore, analyse the results of this equation only. The following results were obtained (figures in brackets denoting standard errors of estimates of buoyancy ratios)[1]:

1. *Total tax revenue:*
   $$\log X_1=\log a+b \log Y$$
   $$\log X_1=-2.027+1.044Y$$
   $$(0.054)$$
   $$R^2=0.966$$

---

1. For all taxes except individual and corporate income tax, the period covered was 1948-63; for these two taxes, figures were available only for the period 1950-62.

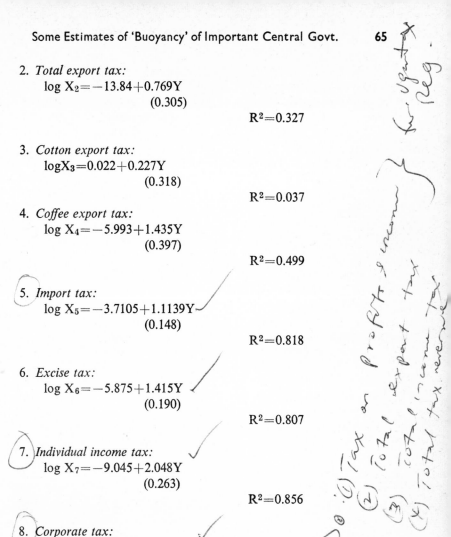

2. *Total export tax:*
   $\log X_2 = -13.84 + 0.769Y$
   $$(0.305)$$

   $R^2 = 0.327$

3. *Cotton export tax:*
   $\log X_3 = 0.022 + 0.227Y$
   $$(0.318)$$

   $R^2 = 0.037$

4. *Coffee export tax:*
   $\log X_4 = -5.993 + 1.435Y$
   $$(0.397)$$

   $R^2 = 0.499$

5. *Import tax:*
   $\log X_5 = -3.7105 + 1.1139Y$
   $$(0.148)$$

   $R^2 = 0.818$

6. *Excise tax:*
   $\log X_6 = -5.875 + 1.415Y$
   $$(0.190)$$

   $R^2 = 0.807$

7. *Individual income tax:*
   $\log X_7 = -9.045 + 2.048Y$
   $$(0.263)$$

   $R^2 = 0.856$

8. *Corporate tax:*
   $\log X_8 = -9.2305 + 2.032Y$
   $$(0.225)$$

   $R^2 = 0.889$

Conclusions:

It will be seen from the above results that the buoyancy ratios for total tax revenue, import and exise duties, individual and corporate income taxes are all greater than one. Individual and corporate income taxes emerge as being especially buoyant, with buoyancy ratios of 2.048 and 2.032 respectively.

Furthermore, in all these cases the 'fit' as represented by the value of coefficient of determination (R^2) is reasonably good; this is of course especially true of total tax revenue where R^2 is 0.996.

If we apply a 95 per cent confidence interval to the buoyancy ratios of these taxes, we find that excise, individual income and corporate taxes still emerge as possessing greater than unity buoyancy. We may, therefore, state with a fair degree of certainty that corporate tax, individual income tax and excise tax have been fairly buoyant in the past.

One cannot draw any firm conclusions from the regression analysis of export taxes, except perhaps the negative conclusion that export taxes show a very poor correlation with income. The main reason for this is that export tax rates are a function of prices and not of export earnings. The values of R^2 are quite low both for export taxes together, and separately for cotton and coffee taxes. Our results (for what they are worth), show that cotton export tax has been the least buoyant of all taxes and is wholly responsible for the low buoyancy of total export taxes. It will be noticed that coffee export tax emerges as fairly buoyant. However, as stated earlier, it is difficult to treat these results with any confidence owing to very poor 'fits' and relatively high standard errors.

Chapter IV

INCOME ELASTICITY OF THE CURRENT TAX STRUCTURE

1. Introduction

In the preceding chapter we analysed the growth and changes in the structure of tax revenue in Uganda in the post-war period. This chapter is concerned with a theoretical evaluation of the income elasticity of the current tax structure in Uganda. The general method employed is to proceed by way of a detailed analysis of the factors influencing the average rate and base of the taxes under consideration. The concluding section draws on this analysis to illuminate the relationship between tax revenue and economic growth.

The income elasticity of a given tax is determined by the relationships among (a) marginal rate of taxation, (b) average rate of taxation, (c) marginal share of tax base in national income, (d) average share of tax base in national income[1]. If the latter

---

1. [Let R stand for revenue from a given tax, B for tax base, Y for national income and e for the income elasticity of the tax.

$$e = \frac{\triangle R}{R} \bigg/ \frac{\triangle Y}{Y}$$

$$= \left(\frac{\triangle R}{R} \bigg/ \frac{\triangle B}{B}\right) \quad \left(\frac{\triangle B}{B} \bigg/ \frac{\triangle Y}{Y}\right)$$

$$= \left(\frac{\triangle R}{\triangle B} \bigg/ \frac{R}{B}\right) \quad \left(\frac{\triangle B}{\triangle Y} \bigg/ \frac{B}{Y}\right)$$

$$\therefore e > I, \text{ if } \left(\frac{\triangle R}{\triangle B} \bigg/ \frac{R}{B}\right) \quad \left(\frac{\triangle B}{\triangle Y} \bigg/ \frac{B}{Y}\right) > I$$

$$\text{or if } \frac{\triangle B}{\triangle Y} = \frac{B}{Y} \text{ and } \frac{\triangle R}{\triangle B} > \frac{R}{B}$$

$$\text{or if } \frac{\triangle R}{\triangle B} = \frac{R}{B} \text{ and } \frac{\triangle B}{\triangle Y} > \frac{B}{Y}$$

$$\text{or if } \frac{\triangle R}{\triangle B} > \frac{R}{B} \text{ by more than } \frac{\triangle B}{\triangle Y} < \frac{B}{Y}$$

$$\text{or if } \frac{\triangle B}{\triangle Y} > \frac{B}{Y} \text{ by more than } \frac{\triangle R}{\triangle B} < \frac{R}{B}$$

remains constant, a given tax will be income elastic provided the marginal exceeds the average rate of taxation; it will have unitary elasticity if the marginal and average rates are equal, and less than unitary elasticity if the marginal falls short of the average rate. Assuming an equality of marginal and average rates, a given tax will be income elastic if the marginal ratio of tax base to national income is greater than the average ratio; and it will be inelastic if the average ratio is greater than the marginal i.e. there is a decline in the share of the tax base in national income. It will, therefore, be seen that it is possible for a tax with a steeply progressive rate structure to have less than unitary elasticity. Conversely, a tax with a regressive rate structure may be income elastic provided the marginal ratio of tax base to national income is sufficiently in excess of the average rate.

In order, therefore, to determine the elasticity of the tax system, it is essential to study in detail the bases and rate schedules of the important taxes in Uganda. We shall be concerned with the export taxes, individual income tax, corporate tax, import duties and excise duties. In the next section we analyze the rate structure of these taxes, reserving for Section III the detailed analysis of tax bases.

II Analysis of the Rate Structure of Some Important Taxes

(i) *Export Taxes*

Export taxes are levied in Uganda on cotton, coffee and hides and skins[1]. The revenue derived from hides and skins is insignificant and will be ignored here.

(a) *Cotton Export Tax*

There are two schedules of export tax rates applicable to the A.R. and B.R. quality of cotton lint. These rates which became effective in April, 1961, are shown in Tables I(a) and I(b). From our point of view, the important characteristic of these taxes is that tax rates vary with the price level and not with the volume of exports. However, before considering them in detail, it may be helpful to make some general points about the factors determining the yield from the cotton export tax; these may be summarized as follows:

---

1. In June, 1964, an export tax on tea was levied at a flat rate of 25 cents per lb.; it was, however, withdrawn a few months later and the revenue collected returned to the growers.

$$^{T}E_c \;=\; f\,(V,P,R)^2$$

The above equation shows that revenue from cotton export tax is a function of the volume and price of cotton exports as well as of the tax rate. Given P and R, $^{T}E_c$ varies proportionately with V i.e. $\dfrac{^{T}E_c}{V}$ (tax per unit of output) is constant. It also means that the average rate of taxation will equal the marginal rate i.e. $\triangle^{T}E_c\,/\,\triangle E_c = {}^{T}E_c\,/\,E_c$; this is shown in Figure 1.

In this situation, the income elasticity of cotton export tax will depend on the relative share of cotton exports in national income; the tax will have a unitary, greater than or less than unitary elasticity according to whether the share of cotton exports in

TABLE I (a)
Cotton lint export duty—A.R. quality

Cts. Per lb. f.o.r.	Duty— Cts. Per lb.	Rate of Duty at Lowest & Highest Price		Average Rates at Median Point
		%	%	%
0 — 50.00	Nil	0	0	0
50.01 — 60.00	2	4.00	3.33	3.64
60.01 — 70.00	3	5.00	4.29	4.62
70.01 — 80.00	4	5.71	5.00	5.33
80.01 — 90.00	6	7.50	6.67	7.06
90.01 — 100.00	9	10.00	9.00	9.47
100.01 — 110.00	11	11.00	10.00	10.48
110.01 — 120.00	13	11.82	10.83	11.30
120.01 — 130.00	15	12.50	11.54	12.00
130.01 — 140.00	17	13.08	12.14	12.59
140.01 — 150.00	19	13.57	12.67	13.10
150.01 — 160.00	21	14.00	13.12	13.55
160.01 — 170.00	23	14.37	13.53	13.94
170.01 — 180.00	25	14.71	13.89	14.29
180.01 — 190.00	27	15.00	14.21	14.59
190.01 — 200.00	29	15.26	14.50	14.87
200.01 — 210.00	31	15.50	14.76	15.12
210.01 — 220.00	33	15.71	15.00	15.35
220 01 — 230.00	35	15.91	15.22	15.56
340.01 — 350.00	59	17.35	16.86	17.10

national income remains constant, rises or falls respectively[3].

On the other hand, given V and R, $^{T}E_c$ will vary directly with P. But the effect of a change in P on the income elasticity of the cotton export tax will depend on the exact relationship between P and the tax

---

2. For an explanation of these and other symbols used in this chapter see "Key to Notation", p. 31.

3. See Footnote 1, page 67.

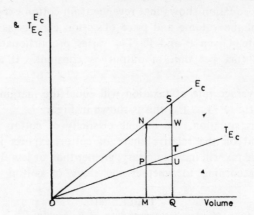

Fig. 1

P and R Constant

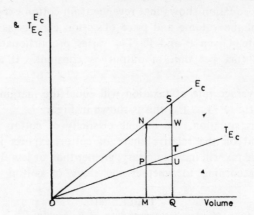

Cotton and	Export Tax	Tax Rates	With Prices Constant

$$\frac{T_{E_C}}{E_C} = \frac{MP}{MN} = \frac{QT}{QS} = \frac{MP+UT}{MN+WS} = \frac{UT}{WS} = \frac{\triangle T_{E_C}}{\triangle E_C}$$

Fig. 2

V and R Constant

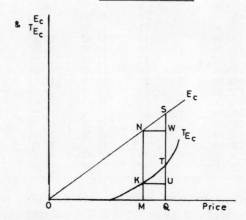

Cotton and	Export Tax	Tax Rates	With Tolume Constant

$$\frac{T_{E_C}}{E_C} = \frac{MK}{MN} \quad < \quad \frac{QT}{QS} = \frac{QU+UT}{QW+WS} = \frac{MK+UT}{MN+SW}$$

$$\therefore \quad \frac{UT}{SW} \quad > \quad \frac{MK}{MN} \quad \text{or} \quad \frac{\triangle T_{E_C}}{\triangle E_C} \quad > \quad \frac{T_{E_C}}{E_C}$$

TABLE I (b)

Cotton lint export duty—B.R. quality

Cts. per lb. f.o.r.		Duty Cts. per lb.	Rate of Duty at Lowest and Highest Price		Average Rate at Median Point
			%	%	%
0.00 —	25.00	2		8	16.00
25.01 —	50.00	3	12	6	8.00
50.01 —	75.00	5	10	6.67	8.00
75.01 —	100.00	7	9.33	7.00	8.00
100.01 —	125.00	8	8.00	6.40	7.11
125.01 —	150.00	10	8.00	6.67	7.27
150.01 —	175.00	12	8.00	6.86	7.38
175.01 —	200.00	14	8.00	7.00	7.47
200.01 —	225.00	16	8.00	7.11	7.53
225.01 —	250.00	18	8.00	7.20	7.58
250.01 —	275.00	20	8.00	7.27	7.62

Provided that when the value is more than 175 cents per pound the duty shall be increased by 2 cents per pound for every increase of 25 cents per pound or part thereof in the value.

per unit. If the ratio of tax to price rises with price increases, then the marginal rate of taxation ($\triangle T_{Ec}/\triangle_{Ec}$) will be an increasing function of P. In this case, export tax will be income elastic provided the share of exports in national income does not fall by a percentage greater than the rise in the rate of taxation i.e. as long as

$\triangle T_{Ec}/\triangle_{Ec} > T_{Ec}/_{Ec}$ by more than $E_c/Y > \triangle E_c/\triangle Y$ Conversely, a rise in the relative share of exports in national income will reinforce the increase in the income elasticity of export tax due to price increases. The situation where tax rates increases with the price level is shown in Figure II.

Our last variable is R, or tax rate schedule. The concept of income elasticity of a given tax implies a constancy of R; hence it is not permissible to vary R. To the extent that the rate schedule is increased or decreased, it will lead to a once-for-all increase or decline in the average rate of taxation. It may also affect the marginal rate of taxation and hence the income elasticity of the tax.

How does the above analysis apply to the export tax on cotton in Uganda? We have seen that the cotton export tax rate varies only with the price level. Therefore, given P and R, $\triangle T_{Ec}/\triangle_{Ec}=T_{Ec}/_{Ec}$, and our earlier remarks about the income elasticity of export taxes in these circumstances apply here. However, as far as the relationship between P and the tax rate is concerned, the last three columns in Table I (a) and I (b) show that the ratio of tax rate to price increases with P for the A.R. Quality and for B.R. Quality it starts rising only after the price has reached a

level of 125.00 cents per lb[4]. The duty on the A.R. Quality Cotton
Lint starts when the price of cotton reaches 50 cents f.o.r. Uganda.
There is a rise of 1, 2 or 3 cents per lb. lint as the price rises from
50 cents to 100 cents per lb. f.o.r. Uganda; after that the duty rises
by 2 cents every 10 cents rise in the price of lint i.e. a constant
marginal rate of 20 per cent.

With the B.R. variety, there is no price floor below which no
duty is levied; the rate rises by 1 or 2 cents per lb. until the price
rises to 125 cents per lb; beyond that level, the duty rises by 2 cents
per lb. for every increase of 25 cents per lb. in the value of cotton
lint i.e. there is a constant marginal rate of 8 per cent in contrast
to the 20 per cent on the A.R. Quality. Furthermore, as the last
columns in Table I(a) and I(b) show, the ratio of tax rate to the
median price starts rising for the B.R. quality lint only when the
price is in excess of the 100-125 cents per lb. range; the same ratio
for the A.R. quality exceeds that for the B.R. quality in the 90-100
cents per lb. price range.

It would, therefore, appear that given V and R, any increase
in the price of A.R. quality lint above 50 cents per lb. will make
$\triangle T_{Ec}/\triangle E_c > T_{Ec}/E_c$, and provided the share of cotton exports
in national income does not fall, will make the tax income elastic.
Similar remarks apply to the tax on the B.R. Quality lint when
its price rises above 125 cents per lb. f.o.r. Uganda. It also follows
that given V, substitution of the A.R. for the B.R. Quality lint,
provided the price level for both is in excess of 90 cents per lb.,
will make $\triangle T_{Ec}/\triangle E_c > T_{Ec}/E_c$, and hence enhance the income
elasticity of export taxes. Our conclusion, therefore, is that given
the constancy of E_c/Y, cotton export taxes are income clastic if E_c
increases at least in part due to an increase in price; they have
unitary income elasticity if E_c increases due exclusively to an
increase in output; and are inelastic if E_c increases despite a fall
in prices. In actual practice, changes in export earnings will be a
function of changes in both the quantity and price of exports.
However, the income elasticity of the export tax on cotton will
depend only on the direction and magnitude of changes in export
prices.

(b) *Coffee Export Tax*

Between April, 1963 and February, 1965 the price "floor"
for Robusta and Arabica coffee was fixed at £90 and £195 per
ton f.o.b. Mombasa respectively. However, in February, 1965 the
"floor" was raised for Robusta to £120. The duty on each ton of

---

4. The great majority of Uganda exports are of the A.R. variety.

coffee is $\frac{1}{3}$ the amount by which the value of such coffee exceeds £120 and £195 per ton f.o.b. respectively for Robusta and Arabica i.e. there is a constant marginal rate of $33\frac{1}{3}$ per cent.

As the tax rate for coffee export tax is sensitive to price only and not to the volume exported, the income elasticity of this tax will be determined by the same factors as that of the cotton export tax. Given P and R, an increase in V (provided the price is above the "floor" level) will lead to a proportionate increase in export tax revenue i.e. $T_{EF}/E_F = \triangle T_{EF}/\triangle E_F$—marginal and average rates are equal. On the assumption that the relative share of coffee exports in the national income does not change, the export tax will have unitary elasticity.

On the other hand, given R and V, an increase in P will make $\triangle T_{EF}/\triangle E_F > T_{EF}/E_F$ and *ceteris paribus*, will make the tax income elastic.

2. *Import Duties*

We have so far been considering export taxes. Increase in income leads to an increase in revenue from outlay taxes through increased expenditure on imports and excisable commodities. In order to determine the income elasticity of outlay taxes, we have to consider the marginal and average rates of taxation with respect to the value of dutiable goods, and the relative share of the latter in national income. As with the taxes on exports, we shall assume that the relative share of imports in national income does not change i.e. $\triangle M/\triangle Y = M/Y$ This assumption will enable us to concentrate on the variables determining the rate of import taxation; it will be removed in the next section.

Revenue from import taxes is a function of the variables summarized below:

$$T_M = f(P, R, V, G)$$

Assuming G, P and R constant, import tax revenue will vary with the volume of imports (V). As the rate of taxation does not vary with V, an increase in V will lead to a similar proportionate increase in T_M i.e. $\triangle T_M/\triangle M = T_M/M$; and other things being equal, import taxes will have unitary income elasticity. We obtain roughly the same result if we allow P to vary, while keeping G,R and V constant. Import taxes will have unitary income elasticity when P alone is allowed to vary only if all prices change in the same proportion and all import duties are on an *ad valorem* basis. The last condition is not satisfied in Uganda where considerable revenue is derived from specific duties on certain imported goods. The existence of specific duties means that the marginal rate of taxation is zero when the prices of commodities subject to specific import duties rise. In a situation like this, an equi-proportionate change in all import prices will make $\triangle T_M/\triangle M < T_M/M$ and hence make the tax inelastic.

Once we assume that all import duties are levied on an *ad valorem* basis, the tax will be inelastic if the price rise experienced by relatively low import duty commodities is higher than the average rise; and it will be elastic if the prices of high import duty commodities rise more than the average price rise.

With P, R and V constant, a change in the composition of imports (G) will also have an effect on import tax revenue; this is because the import duties are not levied at a uniform rate on all imported goods; the effective rates vary from 0 to 300 per cent in the case of Uganda. In general, producers' goods, both intermediate and capital equipment, bear a lower rate of duty than consumer goods. However, there are exceptions to this rule such as fuel, which although partly a producer good, is nevertheless taxed very heavily. Other things being equal, a change in the composition of imports in such a way as to increase the relative importance of heavily taxed commodities will have the effect of making $\triangle T_M/\triangle M > T_M/M$, and hence enhancing the income elasticity of import taxes. Investment boom and the consequent import substitution both have the effect of reducing the relative importance of consumer goods, and hence lowering the elasticity of import taxes.

In an analysis of the income elasticity of import taxes, it is not permissible to vary R; we have seen above that a change in rates will lead to a once-for-all change in T_M/M. Furthermore, a change in rates will almost certainly be accompanied by a change in the other variables determining import revenue, such as the volume of imports. We shall not, therefore, analyse here the revenue implications of a change in import duty rates.

3. *Excise Taxes*

These are levied in Uganda on beer, sugar, cigarettes, tobacco, spirits and matches. The 1964/65 budget added another item to this list—soft drinks. It is the first four commodities mentioned above which have been the most important source of excise tax revenue in the past. It is likely that in future soft drinks will also bring in substantial excise tax revenue. Unlike import duties, the excise duties are specific rather than *ad valorem*, with the result that the revenue from them is a function of the tax rates and quantities of excisable commodities consumed,

$$T_x = f(R_{beer}, \ V_{beer}) \ + \ f(R_{sug.}, \ V_{sug.}) \ + \ f(R_{cig.}, \ V_{cig.})$$

$$+ \ f(R_{tob.}, \ V_{tob.}) \ + \ \cdots\cdots\cdots\cdots$$

On the assumption that the relative share of excisable goods in national income stays constant i.e. $\triangle X/\triangle Y = X/Y$, the income elasticity of excise taxes will be determined by the relationship between the average and marginal rates of excise taxes i.e. by T_X/X and $\triangle T_X/\triangle X$. If prices remain constant, an increase in expenditure on excisable goods will lead to an equal proportionate change in excise tax revenue i.e. $\triangle T_X/\triangle X = T_X/X$, resulting in unitary income elasticity. On the other hand, if prices rise while specific excise duty rates remain constant, $\Delta T_x/\Delta x$ will be zero, and the tax income inelastic; the above result is reversed when prices fall. Thus, unless prices fall, the income elasticity of any one excise tax can never exceed unity; but the elasticity of excise taxes as a whole can exceed unity if the importance of excisable commodities with a higher rate of taxation increases relative to the commodities with a lower rate of taxation.

Apart from that, the buoyancy of excise tax revenue can only be ensured by a progressive rise in specific excise tax rates. We have so far worked on the assumption that the relative share of excisable goods in the national income remains constant. An increase in the latter ratio could also make excise taxes an elastic source of tax revenue.

4. *Individual Income Tax*

We have seen that only a tiny fraction of the working population in Uganda are assessed for income tax. This is because of the relatively high personal and other allowances. Briefly, the following allowances were given in respect of individual income tax in 1963:

(*a*) Single allowance   £225 p.a.

(*b*) Marriage allowance   £700 p.a.

(*c*) Children's allowance   £ 75 for a child under 6 years

£100 for a child between 6 and 12 years.

£150 for a child between 12 and 19 years.

£150 for a child of 17 or over receiving full-time post-secondary education.

(*d*) Insurance allowances—relief is given for life assurance premiums paid and contributions to certain pension schemes up to a maximum of 1/6th of the individual's total income and subject to certain other restrictions and conditions. In general, the first £200 is relieved at not more than Shs. 5

in the £, and any balance at not more than Shs. 2/50 in the £.

It was announced in March, 1965 that the marriage and single allowances have been reduced by £100 and £9 respectively: these changes will apply to the income earned in 1964. It was also decided that relief for life insurance premiums would be granted only on policies expressed in the East African and not foreign currencies. Children's allowances have also been changed with effect from the year of income 1965: £96 each for the first four children and £48 for the fifth and sixth child. The maximum total allowance for children will, therefore, be £480.

Despite these recent changes, the first point to notice about the individual income tax structure is the relatively high exemption limit; a single individual must earn an income which is nine times the average per capita income, and a married person an income which is twenty-five times the per capita income before they become liable to income tax. Judged by these standards, East African countries have some of the highest exemption limits in the world. However, once the individual becomes liable to income tax, the marginal tax rate rises very steeply, starting from 10 per cent for the first £400 of chargeable incomes rising to 75 per cent for chargeable incomes in excess of £9,000. Tables II (a) and II (b) show the marginal and average rates of income taxation respectively at different levels of chargeable income.

It will be noticed from these tables that the marginal rate of taxation rises by 5 per cent irrespective of the size of the 'income slabs'. The result is that the individual income tax is steeply progres-

TABLE II (a)
East African Individual Income Tax: Marginal Rates of Taxation

Total Chargeable Income	ACTUAL RATE					Marginal Rate
£						%
400	First £400 at 2 shg. in the £	..	..	..	..	10
800	Next £400 at 3 shg. in the £	..	..	..	..	15
1200	Next £400 at 4 shg. in the £	..	..	..	..	20
1600	Next £400 at 5 shg. in the £	..	..	..	..	25
2000	Next £400 at 6 shg. in the £	..	..	..	..	30
2500	Next £500 at 7 shg. in the £	..	..	..	..	35
3000	Next £500 at 8 shg. in the £	..	..	..	..	40
4000	Next £1000 at 9 shg. in the £	..	..	..	..	45
5000	Next £1000 at 10 shg. in the £		..	..	..	50
6000	Next £1000 at 11 shg. in the £		..	..	..	55
7000	Next £1000 at 12 shg. in the £		..	..	..	60
8000	Next £1000 at 13 shg. in the £		..	..	..	65
9000	Next £1000 at 14 shg. in the £		..	..	..	70
10,000	Next £1000 at 15 shg. in the £		..	..	..	75

TABLE II (b)
East African Individual Income Tax: Average Rates of Taxation

Chargeable Income	Tax Liability	Tax Liability as a % of Chargeable Income
£	£	%
400	40	10.0
800	100	12.5
1,200	180	15.0
1,600	280	17.5
2,000	400	20.0
2,500	575	23.0
3,000	775	25.8
4,000	1,225	30.6
5,000	1,725	34.5
6,000	2,275	37.9
7,000	2,875	41.1
8,000	3,525	44.1
9,000	4,225	46.9
10,000	4,975	49.8

sive. The average rate of taxation for a person with a chargeable income of £400 is only 10 per cent, rising to 20 per cent for chargeable incomes of £2,000, 35 per cent for chargeable incomes of £5,000 and very nearly 50 per cent for individuals with chargeable incomes of £10,000.

Another property of the income tax relevant to our discussion is the assessment and collection of the tax a year in arrears. This reduces the effectiveness of the stabilizing function of the individual income tax and also makes it less equitable. The government has expressed its intention to introduce a system of P.A.Y.E. as from July, 1966. This will improve both the equity and responsiveness of the tax system in Uganda.

The rate structure of the income tax will also be altered with the introduction of the P.A.Y.E. system. The tax chargeable on individuals will consist of two components: an income tax at the rate of Shs. 2/50 in the £ on all chargeable income, and a surtax at the following rates:

Chargeable Income					Rate
First £1,000	..	..	..	..	.. Nil
Next £1,000	..	..	..	..	.. Shs. 3/- in the £
Next £1,000	..	..	..	..	.. Shs. 5/- in the £
Next £1,000	..	..	..	..	.. Shs. 7/- in the £
Next £1,000	..	..	..	..	.. Shs. 8/- in the £
Next £1,000	..	..	..	..	.. Shs. 9/- in the £
Next £1,000	..	..	..	..	.. Shs. 10/- in the £
Next £3,000	..	..	..	..	.. Shs. 11/- in the £
Excess over £10,000	..	..	..	..	.. Shs. 12/- in the £

Individuals will be subject to surtax but not income tax on dividends received with effect from year of income 1966.

Income Elasticity of Individual Income Tax

Revenue from the individual income tax is a function of the following variables:

$$T_p = f(Y_p, A, R, Y_D, Y_S)$$

Given A, R, and Y_S, an increase in income ($\triangle Y$) will lead to an increase in taxable income ($\triangle Y_p$) only if the former accrues to individuals who are already paying income tax or will enter the tax-paying population by virtue of the increase in their income. If it accrues to individuals in low income brackets, it may not lead to any increase in individual income tax revenue. Furthermore, given $\triangle Y_p$, $\triangle T_p$ will be greater the larger the proportion of $\triangle Y_p$ going to individuals in very high income brackets, in view of the steeply progressive nature of the tax. Thus, the more skewed the distribution of incremental income, the greater the income elasticity of the individual income tax.

The distribution of incremental income between residents and non-residents also has a bearing on the responsiveness of the tax system. It was seen earlier that allowances form a relatively small proportion of non-residents' income, which are therefore taxed at relatively higher rates than similar incomes earned by residents[5]. Thus the greater the proportion of incremental income going to non-residents i.e. the smaller the Y_S, the greater the income elasticity of the fiscal system.

The other two determinants of individual income tax revenue— rates (R) and allowances (A)—are treated as parameters when analyzing the responsiveness of the tax. However, it may be worth considering the revenue effects of changes in tax rate schedules and allowances. An increase in tax rate schedules, *ceteris paribus*, will lead to a once-for-all increase in the ratio T_p/Y, as all the tax-payers will be pushed on to higher tax rates. Similarly, any reduction in allowances will have the effect of a once-for-all increase in T_p/Y, both because this will push the existing tax-payers on to higher marginal tax brackets as well as increase the number of tax-payers. Changes in rate schedules and allowances will also affect the marginal rate of taxation ($\triangle T_p/\triangle Y_p$) · It is, therefore, not possible to say *a priori* what effect these changes will have on the income elasticity of the individual income tax.

---

5. Chapter III, Table XII (*b*).

5. *Corporate Taxation*

This is levied in Uganda on companies, clubs and trusts. One-man firms and partnerships are treated as single individuals for purposes of income tax. There is a slight difference in tax legislation on private or "controlled" companies and public companies. An attempt has been made by legislation to make taxation on "controlled" companies conform as closely as possible to taxation on partnerships or individuals[6]. The basic tax rate on "controlled" companies is Shs. 7/50 in the £ (37½%). In addition, an undistributed income tax at the rate of Shs. 7/50 in the £ is levied unless certain percentages of the total profits are distributed. These percentages vary with the type of business, the current rates are 70 per cent, 80 per cent and 89 per cent. Thus, depending on the type of company, only 30 per cent, 20 per cent and 11 per cent of the net profits are taxed at the standard rate of Shs. 7/50 in the £; the rest, unless they are distributed, are taxed at the penal rate of Shs. 15 in the £ or 75 per cent. The object is to ensure the largest possible distribution of dividends, so that the profits of controlled companies could be taxed as the income of individual shareholders. In view of the maximum rate of tax on undistributed profits in excess of the above percentages, it may be safely presumed that all "controlled" companies retain only the permitted proportion of profits so as not to attract the penal undistributed income tax rate.

There is a slightly different basis of taxation for public companies. A corporation tax is levied on the total net profits of public companies at the rate of Shs. 3/50 in the £ (17½%). This tax cannot be offset against the shareholders' own tax liability. In addition, there is an income tax on public companies amounting to Shs. 4/- in the £ (20%). The recipients of distributed profits are credited with the amount of this income tax which is deducted at source and their tax liability adjusted accordingly. Thus the total tax on undistributed profits is at the rate of Shs. 7/50 in the £ (37½%). On distributed profits, there is a corporation tax of Shs. 3/50 in the £ plus a rate that varies with the individual recipient of dividends according to his total income including dividends.

The 1965/66 Budget has introduced some further changes in company taxes. For the year of income 1965, there will be a single corporation tax of Shs. 7/50 in the £ payable by all companies, whether public or controlled. This tax will not be credited to share-

---

6. For a detailed discussion of this problem, see D. Walker, "A Recent Change in East African Company Taxation", *Public Finance* Vol. XV (No. 2, 1960) pp. 166-188.

holders. The undistributed income tax, levied on controlled companies which fail to distribute a certain percentage of their profits, is to be abolished with effect from the year of income 1965.

The chargeable income of companies on which corporate tax is levied is arrived at after a deduction of depreciation and investment allowances for various classes of capital expenditure. Unfortunately, it has not proved possible to obtain information on the total deduction granted to companies in respect of various allowances.

Income Elasticity of Corporate Taxation

We shall first analyze the income elasticity of the current structure of corporate taxation, leaving for later consideration an analysis of the changes introduced in the 1965/66 Budget.

$$T_c = f(0, R, Y_c, A)$$

The above equation shows that corporate tax revenue is a function of profits, investment and depreciation allowances, tax rate and the division between distributed and retained profits.

We have seen that the undistributed profits of public companies suffer a proportionate tax of $37\frac{1}{2}$ per cent; thus, the average and marginal rate of taxation are equal. Income elasticity of corporate tax, *ceteris paribus*, will therefore be equal to I. The problem is a little more complicated when we make allowance for distributed profits, which are effectively taxed on the chargeable income of the recipients of dividends. If the weighted average of the marginal rate of taxation applicable to all shareholders exceeds 20 per cent, the marginal rate of taxation of corporate income $(\Delta T_c/\Delta 0)$ and hence income elasticity of the tax will be greater under a policy of maximum dividend distribution rather than a maximum retention of profits. It is very likely that the weighted average of the marginal rates of taxation applicable to shareholders will be in excess of 20 per cent as most of them will have chargeable incomes in excess of £800 p.a. Thus a policy of encouraging maximum distribution of profits is desirable in the interests of maximizing tax revenue in the short-run; but such a policy may well conflict with other objectives of fiscal policy such as accelerating the rate of capital formation and eliminating gross inequalities in the consumption pattern of different income groups.

It remains to consider the revenue implications of the distribution of incremental income between the corporate sector (undistributed profits) and individuals ("non-dividend income"). The marginal tax rate on the former is $37\frac{1}{2}$ per cent and on the latter varies from

10 per cent to 75 per cent. $\triangle T/\triangle Y$ will be higher if the incremental income goes to individuals only if the weighted average of their chargeable income is above £2,500—a most unlikely occurrence in Uganda at the present moment. We may, therefore, conclude that from the point of revenue maximization, a policy favouring the more rapid growth of the corporate income vis-à-vis personal income is to be preferred.

We have seen above that as from the year of income 1965 the income tax on companies will be replaced by a corporation tax which is not creditable to shareholders. Assuming a constant share of corporate income in national income, the income elasticity of company taxation will, therefore, be equal to I. The complications arising from the crediting of income tax on companies to shareholders will cease to exist.

III Tax Bases and Economic Growth

The preceding section has analysed the rate structure of some important taxes with a view to determining their income elasticity. In order to round off our discussion it is necessary to subject the tax bases to a similar analysis. We shall be concerned here with the bases of the five most important Central Government taxes viz: cotton and coffee export (E_c and E_F), imports from outside East Africa (M), consumption of excisable goods (X), personal taxable income (^{Y}p) and corporate profits (0). Our task, therefore, reduces itself to an analysis of the effects of economic growth on the relative importance of these tax bases in national income. Our analysis will be theoretical and concern itself with the major determinants of the size of various tax bases. The next chapter attempts to make this exercise more concrete by projecting tax revenue to 1970 on the basis of an assumed pattern and rate of growth of the Uganda economy.

The relative importance of the various tax bases in national income will change as a result of changes in the structure of the economy; the latter in turn will be largely influenced by the strategy of development pursued by the country. In order to make any headway with our analysis, it is essential to consider a variety of patterns of growth of the economy and to work out their effects on the tax bases.

We shall confine our analysis to two dominant patterns of growth. The first one consists of the expansion of primary product exports; this in fact has been the main way in which the Uganda economy has grown in the past. This pattern of growth will be referred to as "export biased growth." In the short-run, expansion of income via increase in primary product exports will inevitably have to come from increases in the two main exports—cotton and coffee. We should further make a distinction between increase in export earnings caused by an increase in the quantity of primary product exports with prices constant (case I), increase in export earnings caused by a rise in export prices (case II), and finally an increase in export earnings despite a fall in export prices (case III) —a pattern more typical of the recent experience in Uganda.

The second route to growth consists in the development of manufactured consumer goods, primarily to replace imports but also to export to other countries. This pattern of growth will be described as "import substitution biased growth." Up till now manufacturing industries have not played a dominant role in the development of the Uganda economy, but it is likely that their importance will increase in the future, though they are unlikely to alter significantly the structure of the economy in the short-run.

It is clear that these patterns of growth are not mutually exclusive and will in actual practice be largely complementary; but it is also true that the planning authorities have the choice of emphasizing the one or the other pattern e.g. the Kenya Plan allocates investment expenditure in such a way as to leave the structure of the economy essentially unchanged, while the Tanganyika Plan aims to reduce the relative importance of exports and to enhance the share of the industrial sector[7]. Our purpose here is to work out the fiscal implications of the alternative strategies of growth; the distinction drawn here between alternative strategies is sharper than is likely to be met in reality, but is designed to bring into relief the major revenue implications of the two extremes in development policy.

What are the implications of these two patterns of growth for the various tax bases? It is not possible to give a precise answer to the question. The outcome will be determined by a variety of complex factors whose exact significance can only be brought out in a detailed, statistical growth model of the economy. All that can be done here is to indicate the major considerations likely to influence the relative size of the various tax bases under the alternative patterns of growth. Under the export biased growth, the prime mover

---

7. See *Kenya Development Plan 1964-70* (Government Printer, Nairobi, 1964); and *Tanganyika Five Year Plan for Economic and Social Development*, 1964-69; Volume I (Government Printer, Dar es Salaam, 1964). For an excellent evaluation of the past and present development plans in East Africa, see P. G. Clark, *Development Planning in East Africa*, (East African Publishing House, Nairobi, 1965.)

in the growth process is an expansion of primary product exports. We should, therefore, expect a rise in the share of exports in national income (E/Y) and if the rise in export earnings is shared by cotton and coffee, E_C/Y and E_F/Y will both rise. The increase in cotton and coffee export earnings may be brought about by an increase in the quantity and prices of exports, or by an increase in one variable adequate to offset the decline in the other.

It is more difficult to be certain about the relative importance of the other tax bases. Imports tend to follow the movements in exports, usually with a few months time lag. An increase in the ratio of export earnings to national income (E/Y) will permit an increase in the ratio of imports to national income (M/Y). The magnitude of the increase in M/Y will depend on, *inter alia*, the pattern of expenditure of recipients of additional income, the diversity and elasticity of supply of domestic manufactures and the effect on the volume of investment. If the export boom is followed by an investment boom, we may expect M/Y to rise sharply because of the large import content of investment expenditure. If, on the other hand, it fails to stimulate investment, M/Y may not rise much.

The effect on the excise tax base will depend on the income elasticity of demand for the main excisable commodities—beer, sugar, cigarettes and tobacco. Unfortunately very little is known about the consumption pattern of different groups of people in East African countries for us to make any meaningful statements about the income elasticities of demand for these commodities. There is evidence provided by the phenomenal growth of beer consumption in the post-war period that it has a high income elasticity of demand; it is doubtful whether the same is true of other excisable goods[8]. Furthermore, since export boom will increase the income primarily of rural dwellers, one may speculate that the elasticities of demand for the excisable goods are unlikely to be high. Consequently, an export biased growth may not increase X/Y.

One can make slightly more definite statements about the

---

8. A study carried out by C. R. Frank concludes that incomes have relatively little effect on sugar consumption in the short-run. The time trend, however, was quite prominent. The period covered—1954-62—was one of relative stagnation of monetary income per head. It is, therefore, likely that Frank's calculations underestimate the income elasticity of demand for sugar; see C. R. Frank, "Analysis and Projection of the Demand for Sugar in East Africa," in *Proceedings of the East African Institute of Social Research Conference*, December 1964.

As for tobacco, there has been a steady and substantial decline in tobacco consumption in the post-war period, partly no doubt due to the substitution of cigarettes for tobacco. This trend is likely to persist in the future, indicating a negative relationship between income and tobacco consumption.

behaviour of income tax bases. Because of the organization of production into small peasant farms and the low level of average income in the agricultural sector, increment in the income of farmers will escape the net of both personal and corporate income tax. Nor is there any reason to believe that the indirect effects of an export boom will necessarily result in a rapid increase in the incomes of persons in higher brackets. We may, therefore, expect a slight decline in Y_P/Y. The corporate tax base, however, is likely to benefit from the generally observed tendency in periods of rapid expansion for profits to rise faster than national income. The exact rise in Y_C/Y will depend on the extent to which the rise in peasant incomes spreads itself to other sectors of the economy. If the multiplier effects of an increase in export earnings are minimized because of leakages through expenditure on imports, Y_C/Y is unlikely to rise much.

Thus export biased growth is likely to raise E_C/Y, E_F/Y, M/Y and Y_C/Y; but it is likely to lower both Y_P/Y and X/Y.

The import substitution biased pattern of growth will have very different effects on the relative importance of the various tax bases. It will obviously be accompanied by a considerable increase in the share of urban incomes. A successful programme of import substitution can only be carried out by a heavy taxation of the agricultural sector and by concentrating investment expenditure on infrastructure, industrial buildings and plant and equipment. We should, therefore, expect a fall in E/Y, and hence in E_C/Y and E_F/Y. If there were no foreign exchange constraint, we would expect a rise in M/Y, caused by the need to obtain from abroad most of the producers' goods necessary to carry out import substitution. Furthermore, the shift of income in favour of urban people will also help to swell the demand for imported consumer goods. But the balance of payments constraint is likely to cause a fall in M/Y.

It is once again difficult to predict the likely change in X/Y. One thing, however, is certain: assuming an equal increase in income, X/Y is likely to be higher under import substitution biased growth than under export biased growth, because the consumption pattern of urban dwellers embodies a larger proportion of excisable goods.

The income tax bases are likely to show the greatest expansion under import substitution biased growth. The main reason for this is that the sectors with the relatively high ratios of taxable income to total income are likely to increase their relative importance in the economy. A programme of industrialization is likely to increase the relative share of the corporate sector; while a rapid increase in urban incomes will help to swell personal taxable incomes.

We may, therefore, conclude that the import substitution pattern of growth is likely to increase both Y_C/Y and Y_P/Y.

IV Tax Revenue and Economic Growth

In this section we shall draw on the preceding analysis to explore the relationship between tax revenue and alternative patterns of growth. We have seen that the income elasticity of the tax system is determined by a weighted average of the income elasticities of component taxes[9]. It would appear that under export-biased growth (case II variety) export taxes will be highly income elastic, both because the marginal rate of taxation $\triangle T_E/\triangle E$ and the marginal ratio of exports to national income $\triangle E/\triangle Y$ will be greater than their average counterparts. Likewise the export-biased growth of the case I variety will make the tax income elastic by increasing the relative share of the export tax base in national income (E/Y).

It is only when export biased growth is brought about by an increase in the volume of exports despite a fall in export prices, that the export taxes may become inelastic; the final outcome will depend on whether the increase in the ratio of tax base to national income (E/Y) is sufficient to offset the decline in the average rate of taxation (T_E/E) as a result of falling prices; if it is not, export taxes will be inelastic.

In the case of the import tax, opposite tendencies are at work: if export boom is followed by an investment boom, it is reasonable to expect a sharp rise in M/Y because of the high import content of investment; at the same time T_M/M is likely to decline because of the relatively lower import duty rates on investment goods under the existing tax structure. The final outcome will clearly depend on the relative strength of these tendencies. If export boom is not followed by an investment boom, M/Y is likely to show a smaller rise, but there is no reason to believe that T_M/M will rise, unless of course the relative importance of manufactured consumer goods in total imports shows an increase. It would, therefore, appear that under export biased growth accompanied by an investment boom, import tax may become income elastic, but is less likely to do so in the absence of an investment boom.

In the case of excise taxes, T_X/X may be expected to decline in a period of rising prices because of the specific nature of these taxes, but as we have seen, X/Y is unlikely to rise. Excise taxes would, therefore, appear to be income inelastic.

---

9. See Footnote 2, Page 2.

As far as individual income is concerned, $^{Y}p/Y$ may be expected to decline because the principal recipients of incremental income—primary product growers—are virtually outside the income tax net; at the same time $^{T}p/^{Y}p$ is unlikely to rise because of the expected movement towards more even distribution of income as a result of the decline in the relative importance of the incomes of the immigrant races. It thus seems that individual income tax is likely to prove inelastic. Corporate tax, on the other hand, should be income elastic because of the likely increase in $^{Y}c/Y$.

We may sum up our discussion by saying that under export-biased growth, export and corporate taxes are likely to be income elastic, while excise and individual income tax are likely to be inelastic. Import tax may also be elastic under some favourable conditions. In the absence of any quantitative relationships, it is difficult to say whether the tax system as a whole is likely to be income elastic. However, in view of the considerable importance of export taxes in the Uganda tax system, an export-biased pattern of growth if accompanied by a boom in export prices, may be expected to make the tax system elastic.

Under import substitution-biased growth, many of the above relationships are likely to be reversed. Export taxes may be expected to become inelastic because of a likely decline in E/Y, unless T_E/E rises adequately to offset it. The latter will rise only if there is an increase in export prices.

With regard to import taxes, it was shown earlier that M/Y may be expected to decline because of the foreign exchange constraint; at the same time T_M/M is certain to fall owing to changes in the composition of imports, resulting in a substantial relative increase in intermediate and investment goods and a relative decline in consumer goods. Import taxes may, therefore, be expected to prove income inelastic under an import substitution pattern of growth.

Excise taxes may also prove income inelastic for the reasons mentioned when discussing their elasticity under export-biased growth namely—a decline in the average rate of taxation and a probable relative contraction of the tax base. The decline in the tax base is, however, likely to be much less under import substitution than under export-biased pattern of growth because of the greater importance of urban incomes in the former.

Both individual and corporate income tax are likely to be highly income elastic under import substitution pattern of growth because of a certain relative expansion of their tax bases. Corporate tax has a proportionate rate structure; but in the case of individual

income tax, a rise in Y_p/Y could be offset to some extent by a fa.
in T_p/Y_p, caused by a greater equality of income distribution.

To sum up our discussion, under import substitution pattern
of growth, export and import taxes are likely to be income inelastic;
excise taxes may also prove inelastic; while individual and corporate
income taxes are likely to be income elastic. As for the tax system
as a whole, it would appear that with export and import taxes
becoming inelastic, the tax system is likely to be inelastic. The
buoyancy of corporate and individual income tax, because of their
relatively small importance in the Uganda tax system, is unlikely
to offset the inelasticity of the two major taxes.

It would also appear from the above analysis that the total
tax revenue is likely to be more elastic (or less inelastic) under the
export-biased as compared with the import substitution-biased
pattern of growth. The most important reason for this is that under
the latter growth pattern there is likely to be a relative contraction
of two important tax bases—cotton and coffee exports and imports—
and a change in the composition of imports resulting in a reduction
in the average rate of import taxation. At the same time, there is
in the present Uganda tax structure, no comprehensive sales tax
which will bring within the tax net the base that is likely to expand
most rapidly, i.e. consumption of domestically produced goods and
services.

In conclusion, it may be remarked that in the absence of
quantitative date on the growth of the economy, an analysis of
the income elasticity of a tax system must inevitably be highly
abstract and tentative. The next chapter attempts to remedy this
deficiency by calculating the responsiveness of the Uganda tax
system to increases in income on the basis of an assumed pattern
and rate of growth of the economy.

Chapter V

PROJECTION OF TAX REVENUE TO 1970

I Introduction

In this chapter we shall develop a method for making medium-term projections of tax revenue. The application of this method is illustrated by reference to a statistical growth model of the Uganda economy. Although our results throw some light on the responsiveness of the Uganda fiscal system and are, therefore, of interest in their own right, our main contribution consists in developing an operational method for projecting tax revenue in a growing economy.

The importance of an exercise of this kind is self-evident. Revenue projection ought to be an integral part of any development plan, for it shows the resources likely to be available to the state through taxes for the financing of the plan. Unfortunately, most development plans, and this is especially true of the development plans of the East African countries, contain only a perfunctory analysis of the fiscal implications of the rate and pattern of growth assumed in the plans. It is, therefore, not surprising that inadequacy of domestic finance should prove a crucial constraint on the implementation of development plans in many developing countries[1]. Part of the reason for the relative neglect of fiscal policy in development plans undoubtedly lies in the extreme difficulty of making forecasts of tax revenue over the plan period. Yet the successful implementation of the plan is so closely dependent on the availability of adequate finance that, as a first step towards designing an appropriate tax structure for rapid growth, an attempt must be made to work out the fiscal implications of the strategy of development embodied in the plan.

We attempt to project tax revenue to 1970 on the basis of the existing structure of central government taxation and on the assumption that the Uganda economy follows the growth path charted

---

1. See P. G. Clark, "Foreign Aid, Domestic Finance and the Development Plan". *Proceedings, University of East Africa Conference on Foreign Aid* (Dar es Salaam), forthcoming.

in a statistical model by P.G. Clark and B. Van Arkadie[2]. The Clark-Van Arkadie model has been used for two reasons: in the first place, the initial plan framework for the second Five Year Plan of Uganda broadly resembles the model projections, and therefore the effort at revenue projection is not entirely an academic exercise but may well have considerable policy implications. Secondly, this is the only model available which spells out in sufficient detail the structural changes in various sectors of the economy necessitated by a certain strategy of development to enable us to make tax revenue projections. It must, however, be emphasized that we are not "wedded" to any of the figures used here; indeed some of the quantitative assumptions made here may appear highly dubious, or even positively wrong. As mentioned earlier, all that is claimed here is a modest contribution towards devising a method for projecting revenue in countries possessing a tax structure similar to that of East African countries.

The next section contains the salient features of the statistical projection model being used here; this is followed by a projection of individual Central Government tax sources. In the concluding section we bring together our projections to throw some light on the nature and elasticity of the Uganda fiscal system.

II The Statistical Projection Model of the Uganda Economy

Before proceeding with the task of revenue projection it is essential to give a brief description of the statistical projection model of the Uganda economy constructed by Clark and the resultant use of the model made by Clark and Van Arkadie to illustrate the pattern and rate of growth necessary to double per capita output in Uganda in fifteen years[3]. We shall only emphasize those features of the projection model which are relevant to our analysis. The key features of the model may best be described in the words of its author: "First, it is a sector model distinguishing six producing sectors of the economy, seven kinds of imports, two classes of exports, four forms of capital formation, four kinds of government

2. P. G. Clark and B. Van Arkadie, "Development Goals for the Uganda Economy in 1981", *Economic Development Research Project Paper No. 42* (this article forms chapter V of a book by P. G. Clark, *Development Planning in East Africa* (East African Publishing House, Nairobi 1965) also see P. G. Clark, "The Rationale and Uses of a Projection Model of the East African Economies," *East African Economic Review* (June 1965).

3. For a detailed description of the characteristics and operation of the statistical projection model for the Uganda economy, see P. G. Clark, "The Rationale and Uses of a Projection Model for the East African Economies," *op. cit.* For further details of the conditions necessary for a doubling of output per head in Uganda in fifteen years, see P. G. Clark, *Development Planning in East Africa, op. cit.*

taxes, and certain other variables. Thus it embodies substantially more specific information than a purely aggregative model but still much less detail than is involved in planning development actions within ministries. Second, it portrays an economy in which everything depends, by way of the structural relationships among its parts, upon five autonomous factors: the real quantity of agricultural exports, the prices of those exports, the value of manufactured exports, import substitution in manufactured products, and central government current expenditures. In particular, it specifies that required capital formation is derived within the model from implied increases in domestic production. Third, the parameters describing the structural relationships among parts of economy must each be projected into the future. Some are assumed to remain unchanged or to follow a time-trend, while others are assumed to be adjustable by government policy. Fourth, it is a linear model; capital formation, though in principle non-linear, is represented by a linear approximation depending on a tentative initial estimate of rate of growth. Thus though the algebra is somewhat laborious, it is mathematically simple. Finally, the model is designed to emphasize three potential constraints on development expenditures and policies: the balance of trade, which depends mainly on the various imports parameters; the government budget surplus or deficit, which depends mainly on the tax revenue parameters; and the required savings, which depends mainly on the capital formation parameters."[4]

TABLE I
Structure of the Uganda Economy: 1962 and 1970

Sector	1962: £m.	% of G.D.P.	Growth rate % p.a.	1970 £m.	% of G.D.P.
Monetary Gross Domestic Product ..	107.5	—	8.2	201.4	—
			6.6	180.0	—
Agricultural Product	49.9	46.4	6.7	81.3	40.4
			5.3	75.4	41.9
Construction Product	3.9	3.6	15.7	12.5	6.2
			11.5	9.3	5.2
Manufacturing Product	8.6	8.0	10.6	19.3	9.6
			6.9	14.7	8.2
Services Product ..	24.9	23.2	8.9	49.3	24.5
			7.2	43.4	24.1
Government Product	12.4	11.5	8.1	24.9	12.4
			8.1	24.9	13.8
Transport Product ..	7.8	7.3	7.7	14.1	7.0
			5.8	12.3	6.8

Note: The upper line opposite sectoral products shows the structure of the economy if it grows at 8.2 per cent p.a.; the lower line refers to a 6.6 per cent p.a. growth rate.

---

4. Clark, *op. cit.*, p. 2.

It must be mentioned further that six producing sectors (agriculture, construction, manufacturing, services, government, transport), seven kinds of imports (food, manufactured consumer goods, vehicles, intermediate goods, fuel, construction material, equipment), and two classes of exports (agricultural and non-agricultural), are arrived at after a considerable reclassification of the official statistics and represent an attempt at an economically more significant classification of some important sectors.

On the basis of this statistical model, Clark and Van Arkadie show the various structural changes that will be necessary if the goal of doubling per capita income is to be achieved in fifteen years. This implies a cumulative growth rate of 8.2 per cent p.a. in monetary G.D.P.; the authors, however, also go on to chart the probable growth path of the economy if it grows at a lower rate of 6.6 per cent p.a. Many would consider the 8.2 per cent p.a. growth rate, accepted provisionally as an official target in the Second Five Year Plan of Uganda, as unattainably high. We have, therefore, decided to make two projections of tax revenues, corresponding to the 8.2 per cent and 6.6 per cent p.a. growth rates of monetary G.D.P. The strategy of development embodied in the sectoral projections of the growth model corresponds very roughly to what we have called an import substitution biased pattern of growth; this is especially true of the growth path followed under the assumption of the 8.2 per cent p.a. growth rate. Table I shows the projected values of the various sectors in the economy. We discuss below in detail some of these important sectoral changes. Here we need only say that they imply a sharp increase in the share of capital formation in national income; a relative decline in the share of agriculture and agricultural exports in the economy; a rise in the share of most other sectors, especially of construction and manufacturing; a change in the composition of imports and exports, with an increase in the share of equipment and construction in the import bill, and a slight reduction in the share of agricultural exports in total exports.

In order to use this model for projection of tax revenue, we have had to modify it in some respects. In the first place, the time period relevant for our analysis is 1962-70, rather than 1981. In their projections, Clark and Van Arkadie assume a lower growth rate in the earlier phase, accelerating to a higher rate later in the period. In our analysis we have assumed that the economy will grow at a rate of 8.2 per cent p.a. (and 6.6 per cent under the less ambitious growth rate assumption) between 1962 and 1970. Secondly, for our purposes we are only interested in imports from outside East Africa, as imports from the other East African countries are admitted duty-free; Clark and Van Arkadie lump together inter-territorial and foreign imports. We have attempted to separate foreign imports from total imports by assuming that both types of imports grow at the rates assumed in the growth model. It may be objected that in the past inter-territorial trade has expanded at a much faster rate than foreign trade, and thus our assumption of equal growth rates for both types of imports will overstate the proceeds from import taxes. To this objection it may be replied that the recent modifications in the working of the East African common market will have the effect of slowing down the rate of growth of inter-territorial trade; furthermore, the pattern of future imports assumed in the projections made here is such that a larger proportion of imports will have to come from outside East Africa.

Lastly, whereas the projections contained in the Clark-Van Arkadie growth model are based on the assumption of a substantial increase in the ratio of tax revenue to monetary G.D.P. to finance greatly increased public investment programme, we shall proceed on the assumption of an unchanged tax structure since our basic purpose is to make projections of tax revenue on the basis of existing tax structure and hence to calculate its income elasticity[5]. This procedure may appear highly unsatisfactory, but we can meet at least part of the objection by assuming that the increase in public investment which in the growth model is supposed to be financed by tax revenue is in fact financed through domestic loans. While the incentive effects of these two methods of raising revenue may clearly be different, they achieve the same objective in so far as their effect on private disposable incomes is concerned. With these qualifications we can now proceed to our main task of making revenue projections from individual tax sources as well as from the tax system as a whole on the basis of a projected pattern and rate of growth of the Uganda economy to 1970.

---

5. As we are comparing tax revenues in 1962 with those projected for 1970, the reference to the existing structure is meant to refer to the 1962 tax structure. There have been some increases in import and excise duty rates in 1963, 1964 and 1965; also, as mentioned in the last chapter, personal allowances in respect of income tax have been reduced slightly for the 1964 assessment of income tax. But these are relatively minor changes; the tax structure today remains essentially the same as it was three years ago. To make an allowance for these changes would have greatly complicated the task of comparing 1962 with 1970 tax revenue, without contributing in any significant way to an improvement in our method of tax projection or to a better understanding of the responsiveness of the Uganda fiscal system. We therefore decided not to include this refinement in our projections.

III Projection of Tax Revenue

We shall attempt projections of import duties, export taxes, excise duties, individual and corporate income taxes and all other Central Government taxes (mostly licences). The general method followed is to derive the value of various tax bases from the projections of growth of the Uganda economy, and to derive tax rates by making suitable assumptions about the likely trends of the factors affecting rates for various taxes.

(1) *Import Tax Revenue*

We make two sets of projections of import tax revenue, corresponding to the two assumed rates of growth of monetary G.D.P.— 8.2 per cent and 6.6 per cent p.a. The first step in our calculations must be an estimate of import bill in 1970. According to the Clark-Van Arkadie projections, imports will increase by the same rate—7 per cent p.a.—whether the economy grows at the faster or the relatively slower rate of 6.6 per cent p.a. As mentioned earlier we are only interested in imports from outside East Africa. Table II shows the total value as well as the composition of imports in 1970, calculated according to the growth rates for various categories of imports assumed in the Clark-Van Arkadie projections. It will

TABLE II
Composition of foreign net imports: 1962 and 1970

Category of imports	1962 £m.	% of imports	Growth rate % p.a.	1970: £m.	% of imports
Food imports	1.8	6.8	4.2	2.50	5.5
			5.8	2.83	6.2
Manufactured consumer imports	10.7	40.7	4.2	14.87	32.8
			5.7	16.67	36.6
Vehicle imports	2.6	9.9	8.0	4.81	10.6
			6.3	4.24	9.3
Intermediate imports	2.6	9.9	6.0	4.14	9.1
			6.8	4.39	9.6
Fuel imports ..	2.3	8.7	8.5	4.42	9.8
			6.9	3.92	8.6
Construction material imports ..	1.4	5.3	5.8	2.20	4.9
			10.1	3.02	6.6
Equipment imports	4.9	18.6	12.3	12.39	27.3
			9.9	10.43	22.9
Total imports ..	26.3	100.0	7	45.33	
			7	45.50	
Imports/monetary G.D.P.	24.5%			22.5% 25.3%	

Notes: 1, The upper line opposite each category of imports refers to the rate of growth of imports under 8.2 per cent p.a. growth rate; the lower line refers to 6.6 per cent p.a. growth rate.

2. Total imports in both cases should be £45.20m; the slight divergence from this figure is due to rounding.

be seen that imports as a proportion of monetary G.D.P. fall from 24.5 per cent in 1962 to 22.5 per cent in 1970 on the assumption of an 8.2 per cent p.a. growth rate; on the alternative hypothesis of a less ambitious growth rate, imports as a proportion of monetary G.D.P. will rise from the 1962 level to 25.3 per cent. This difference is due to a higher share of investment in G.D.P. and much higher import substitution rates under an 8.2 per cent p.a. growth rate. Table II shows the changes in the composition of imports between 1962 and 1970[6]. Under the 8.2 per cent growth rate, there is a sharp increase in the share of equipment from 18.6 per cent in 1962 to 27.3 per cent of total imports in 1970, a sharp decline in the share of manufactured consumer goods from 40.7 per cent to 32.8 per cent. Furthermore, imports of food, intermediate goods and construction materials suffer a slight relative decline, while vehicle imports and fuel increase slightly in relative importance. If, on the other hand, we assume a 6.6 per cent growth rate, the increase in the share of equipment is not so marked nor the decline in the share of manufactured consumer goods so steep. Also, apart from construction materials, all other categories of imports suffer a slight decline in relative importance. These changes in imports are of course a reflection of the structural changes in the economy implied by the alternative growth rates. In particular, the 8.2 per cent growth rate assumes a much higher degree of import substitution.

The next step in our analysis is to calculate the average rate of import duty on the different categories into which imports are classified. The results of this exercise for 1962 are shown in Table III (a). It will be noticed that the highest rates of duty are levied on fuel (92%), food (48%) and manufactured consumer goods (30%), while the lowest rates are levied on equipment (4%), construction materials (7%) and intermediate imports (12%). On the assumption of an unchanged import tax structure, we can obtain estimates of import tax revenue in 1970 under the alternative hypotheses about the rate of growth of the economy. Our calculations, summarized in Table III (a), show that proceeds from import duty rise to £11.65m. in 1970 under the 8.2 per cent growth rate and to £11.81m. under the 6.6 per cent growth rate, as compared with £7.19m. in 1962. Table III (b) further shows that import tax revenue as a proportion of monetary G.D.P. (T_M/Y) declines from 6.68 per cent in 1962 to 6.56 per cent and 5.78 per cent in 1970,

---

6. The import categories used here have been arrived at after considerable transfer among S.I.T.C. classes of imports.

TABLE III (a)
Import tax rates and import tax revenue: 1962 and 1970

Category of imports	Tax rates	Tax revenue 1962: £m.	Tax revenue 1970: £m.
Food imports	0.48	0.87	1.20
			1.36
Manufactured consumer imports ..	0.30	3.21	4.46
			5.00
Vehicle imports	0.16	0.43	0.77
			0.68
Intermediate imports	0.12	0.31	0.50
			0.53
Fuel imports	0.92	2.08	4.07
			3.61
Construction Material imports ..	0.07	0.10	0.15
			0.21
Equipment imports	0.04	0.19	0.50
			0.42
TOTAL TAX REVENUE		7.19	11.65
			11.81

Note: The upper line opposite each category of imports refers to tax revenue if the economy grows at 8.2 per cent p.a.; the lower line refers to 6.6 per cent p.a. growth rate.

TABLE III (b)
Import duty yield relative to G.D.P.

Year	M/Y	T_M/M	T_M/Y
1962	0.245	0.273	0.0668
1963	0.240	0.299	0.0718
1970 : 8.2 per cent growth rate ..	0.225	0.257	0.0578
1970 : 6.6% growth rate	0.253	0.260	0.0656

Note: Values of M/Y, T_M/M, T_M/Y for 1962 and 1963 differ from those shown in Table VIII, Chapter III, because of the difference in the definition of the import base; there we used retained imports (imports minus re-exports) as our base, whereas in this table our base is imports inclusive of re-exports.

corresponding to 6.6 per cent and 8.2 per cent rates of growth. This decline is due to a combination of two factors: under the more ambitious growth rate, the relative importance of imports in the economy declines between 1962 and 1970; secondly the category of imports experiencing the highest growth—equipment—is also the one with the lowest rate of import duties. Food and manufactured consumer goods which suffer a slight relative decline are also among the most heavily taxed imports. T_M/Y does not decline as much with a lower growth rate both because the share of equipment does not rise so sharply, and also because the increase in M/Y offsets, to some extent, the decline in the average rate of import taxation (T_M/M). With an 8.2 per cent growth rate, the decline in M/Y reinforces the effect of a fall in T_M/M to bring down T_M/Y.

If we take 1963 as the base year the decline in T_M/Y under either of the growth rates is less marked; this is because M/Y in

1963 was lower than in 1962, and also because the average rate of import duties on equipment in 1963 was substantially higher than in 1962. Thus although using 1963 figures reduces the estimated fall in T_M/Y, it does not reverse the direction of the change. Our conclusion must, therefore, be that under the 1962-63 structure of import duties, rapid economic growth on the lines charted in the Clark-Van Arkadie projection model will lead to a decline in T_M/Y; in other words, import taxes have an income elasticity of less than 1.

(2) *Export Taxes*

It is much more difficult to make realistic projections of export tax revenue. This is because both the base as well as the average rate of export taxes are influenced by factors such as weather conditions and world commodity prices which are inherently unpredictable. In our projections we have made assumptions, as best as we can, on the basis of past trends and future economic conditions and policies, about the likely trends in the volume and price of cotton and coffee exports. It cannot be over-emphasized that if the world economic conditions turn out to be very different from those envisaged in these projections, our calculations would turn out to be all wrong.

The Clark-Van Arkadie model projects agricultural export earnings to 1981 on the basis of a 4 per cent p.a. growth rate since 1963. With the less ambitious growth rate, agricultural export earnings are estimated to increase by 3.1 per cent p.a. The growth in real agricultural exports is higher, as these projections assume a downward price trend of 1 per cent p.a. In order to enable us to make projections of cotton and coffee export taxes separately, we have to make specific assumptions not only about the overall growth rate of agricultural exports but also about their cotton and coffee components. The details of these calculations are shown in Table IV (*a*). Some of the important assumptions must, however, be mentioned here. We assume that, owing to the International Coffee Agreement, coffee prices, both Robusta and Arabica, will stabilize at their 1963 level; thus our 1970 prices are the same as in 1963. As far as Robusta Coffee is concerned, prices in 1963 were substantially higher than in the period 1960-62; on the other hand, they were much lower than the ruling prices throughout the fifties. Robusta prices moved sharply upwards in 1964, but have now declined below the 1963 level. All things being considered, the assumption that prices will eventually stabilize at their 1963 level seems as realistic as any other.

We further assume that the quantity of coffee exported will increase at the rate of 2 per cent p.a. between 1963 and 1970 under both alternative rates of growth starting from an average of 1962-64 exports. This, of course, is a substantially lower growth rate of the quantity exported than achieved in the past. The justification for this assumption is that under the International Coffee Agreement exports of coffee from Uganda are subject to a quota, which is unlikely to be increased by an average of more than 2-3 per cent p.a. Furthermore, in order to avoid the accumulation of large coffee surpluses, the government policy has been altered to discourage the production of coffee and to encourage the production of cotton and other crops.

TABLE IV (a)

Projection of export tax revenue

		Projected values in 1970	
		assuming 8.2% growth rate	assuming 6.6% growth rate
Cotton:			
Quantity exported (centals)	1,377,393[1]	2,071,048[2]	1,938,267[3]
Price (cts. per lb.)	223[4]	200.7[5]	200.7[5]
Exports (£m)		20.8	19.5
Export tax rate at the 1962 tax schedule		0.144	0.144
Tax revenue		3.0	2.8
Robusta Coffee:			
Quantity exported (tons)	127,394[6]	146,337[7]	146,337[7]
Price (£ per ton)	182.3[8]	182.3[8]	182.3[8]
Exports (£m)		26.7	26.7
Export tax rate at the 1962 tax schedule		0.114	0.114
Tax revenue		3.04	3.04
Arabica Coffee:			
Quantity exported (tons)	10,250[6]	11,774[7]	11,774[7]
Price (£ per ton)	265[8]	265[8]	265[8]
Export tax rate at the 1962 tax schedule		0.0879	0.0879
Tax revenue (£m)		0.24	0.24
Total coffee export tax revenue (£m)		3.24	3.24
Total export tax revenue (£m)		6.24	6.04

Notes: 1. Average of 1961, 1963, 1964. The quantity exported in 1962 is excluded because it was abnormally low.
2. Assumes a 6 per cent p.a. growth rate between 1963 and 1970.
3. Assumes a 5 per cent p.a. growth rate between 1963 and 1970.
4. Average export price in 1962, 1963, 1964.
5. Assumes a 10 per cent price decline between 1962-64 and 1970.
6. Average of 1962, 1963, 1964.
7. Assumes a 2 per cent p.a. growth rate.
8. Average price in 1963; it is assumed to stay constant.

With regard to cotton, we assume that the quantity exported will increase at the rate of 6 per cent or 5 per cent p.a. between 1963 and 1970, depending on the overall rate of growth of economy, and starting from an average of the quantity of cotton exported in 1961, 1963 and 1964.[7] This assumption once again is at variance with the trend in the post-war period. The rationale for this assumption of a substantially higher growth rate than achieved in the past is relatively better price prospects for cotton than for coffee, an increased emphasis in governmental policy towards cotton production, and the inability to increase coffee exports owing to the quota system operated under the International Coffee Agreement. The success of this policy can be seen in a record cotton crop expected in the 1964/65 season. As far as cotton export price is concerned, we assume a 10 per cent decline between 1962-64 and 1970. This assumption is justified by the price trend in the late fifties and early sixties and is also in conformity with the projections made by independent studies such as those by the Food and Agricultural Organization.

On the basis of the above projections of the prices and quantities of cotton and coffee exported in 1970, it is a simple matter to calculate export tax revenue. This is done in Table IV (*a*), which estimates export tax revenue from cotton and coffee in 1970 at £6.24m. and £6.04m, corresponding to the 8.2 per cent and 6.6 per cent p.a. growth rates of monetary incomes. The projection of coffee export tax revenue is the same under both growth rates because of the assumptions made. However, export tax revenue from cotton is expected to be slightly higher under the 8.2 per cent p.a. growth rate.

Table IV (*b*) shows that the ratio of export tax revenue to monetary G.D.P. (T_E/Y) is calculated at 3.10 per cent in 1970 under an 8.2 per cent p.a. growth rate, and at 3.36 per cent under a lower growth rate. This compares with 2.32 per cent and 4.51 per cent in 1962 and 1963 respectively and with 4.19 per cent for 1962-64. Therefore, compared with 1963, T_E/Y shows a considerable decline; but it represents an increase over 1962. However, as mentioned earlier, 1962 must be seen as an abnormal year because of an abnormally reduced cotton crop. Table IV (*b*) further shows that under 8.2 per cent growth rate, E_C/Y falls from an average of 11.11 per cent in 1963, to 10.33 per cent in 1970, while E_F/Y falls more sharply from 21.21 per cent in 1962-64 to 14.60 per cent

---

7. We have excluded 1962 because of the abnormally low exports of cotton that year owing to adverse weather conditions.

TABLE IV (b)
Cotton and coffee export tax yield relative to G.D.P.

Year	E_C/Y	T_{E_C}/E_C	T_{E_C}/Y	E_F/Y	T_{E_F}/E_F	T_{E_F}/Y	E/Y	T_E/E	T_E/Y
1962-64[1] ..	0.1223	0.1179	0.0142	0.2121	0.1296	0.0287	0.3120	0.1297	0.419
1962	0.0769	0.1723	0.0133	0.1872	0.0530	0.0099	0.2641	0.0878	0.0232
1963	0.1111	0.1350	0.0150	0.2113	0.1423	0.0301	0.3224	0.1399	0.0451
1970 (8.2% growth rate)	0.1033	0.1445	0.0149	0.1460	0.1102	0.0161	0.2493	0.1243	0.0310
1970 (6.6% growth rate)	0.1081	0.1445	0.0156	0.1633	0.1102	0.0180	0.2714	0.1238	0.0336

1. For cotton, average of 1961, 1963, 64; for Coffee, average of 1962, 1963, and 1964. Figures of Export tax revenue in 1964 are an average of actual revenue in 1963/64 and revised estimates for 1964/65.

in 1970. The decline in E_C/Y and E_F/Y is less under the 6.6 per cent growth rate. Lastly, the average rate of coffee export taxes (T_{E_F}/E_F) in 1970 at 11.02 per cent is higher than in 1962 but lower than in 1963 or the average of 1962-64. The reason for this is that 1970 prices are assumed to be higher than 1962 prices; on the other hand, the tax rate schedule assumed is the one which was prevalent in 1962, rather than in 1963[8]. As for cotton, T_{E_C}/E_C in 1970 at 14.45 per cent is higher than in 1963 but lower than the average of 1961, 1963 and 1964. It should really be lower than in 1963 as well, but due to our method of calculating average tax revenue, the value of T_{E_C}/E_C in 1963 is underestimated and in 1962 overestimated.[9]

(3) *Excise Taxes*

As excise taxes are levied on a specific basis, we need to find a way of projecting the consumption of main excisable commodities to 1970. This was done by a regression of the consumption of excisable goods on disposable income and a time variable, on the basis of data available for the period 1954-63.[10] We used an equation of the following type:

$C = a_0 + a_1 Y_d + a_2 t$ where Y_D stands for disposable income, c for the consumption of individual excisable commodities, t for a trend factor and a_0, a_1 and a_2 are constants.

Having obtained the values for these constants for the three excisable commodities—beer, sugar and cigarettes—it was a simple matter to project the consumption of these commodities in 1970 and hence to calculate the excise tax revenue in 1970, assuming the 1962 excise tax structure. Tobacco is in a special position as its consumption is apparently completely unrelated to disposable income. On the basis of the past trends in tobacco consumption, it was considered reasonable to project consumption of 450,000 lbs. for the year 1970. Likewise we assume that revenue from other goods (matches, spirits etc) will amount to £75,000 in 1970 under an 8.2 per cent growth rate and £65,000 under a 6.6 per cent growth rate.

8. Until February 1963, the price "floor" for export tax on Robusta was £120 per ton f.o.b. Mombasa. It was then lowered to £90 per ton; hence the higher average rate of coffee tax in 1963. However, it was again raised to £120 per ton in February, 1965.

9. See footnote 7, page 35.

10. It is only fair to mention that from 1954 to 1962 monetary incomes were relatively stagnant in Uganda; the use of income elasticity coefficients derived from this period in a time of rapidly increasing incomes may tend to introduce a downward bias in our projection.

Tables V(a) and (b) show the details of our calculations[11]. These tables show that excise tax revenue in 1970 is estimated to amount to £4.82m. and £4.57m., corresponding to the two rates of growth of the economy. Furthermore, it will be noticed that the relative importance of excise tax revenue (T_x/Y) declines somewhat under the 8.2 per cent growth rate from 2.69 per cent in 1962 (and 2.89 per cent in 1963) to 2.39 per cent in 1970[12]. If we assume a lower growth rate of 6.6 per cent p.a., T_x/Y suffers a lesser decline to 2.54 per cent. The main reason for a lesser relative decline under a lower growth rate is that, as shown by the regression equations, the consumption of all these commodities, but especially of beer and sugar, is strongly influenced by non-income factors such as the trend and "autonomous" factors. The retail prices of most excisable commodities changed relatively little during the period 1954-63, except perhaps for the last year; so it is unlikely   that

TABLE V (a)
Projection of excise tax revenue under 8.2% growth rate

We used a regression equation of the following type:
$$C = a_0 + a_1 Y_d + a_2 t$$
where C stands for consumption, Y_d for disposable income, t for a trend factor and a_0, a_1, a_2 are constants. The period analyzed was 1954-63. For 1970, the value of $t = 16$ and $Y_d = 162.6$

(1) *Revenue from beer:*
   Projected beer consumption ('000 standard gallons) in 1970 is given by:
$$C = 531.56 + 6.1232Y_d + 90.595t$$
$$R^2 = 0.575$$

	$= 2976.712$
Tax rate in 1962	$= £0.339$ per standard gallon
∴ Tax revenue in 1970	$= £1.009$m.

(2) *Revenue from sugar:*
   Projected sugar consumption ('000 cwts) in 1970 is given by:
$$C = 159.31 + 9.9489Y_d + 41.148t$$
$$R^2 = 0.93$$

	$= 2435.369$
Tax rate in 1962	$= £0.667$ per cwt.
Revenue in 1970	$= £1.617$m.

(3) *Revenue from cigarettes:*
   Projected cigarettes consumption ('000 lbs) in 1970 is given by:
$$C = 880.98 + 13.362Y_d + 2.0411t$$
$$R^2 = 0.86$$

	$= 3086.299$
Tax rate in 1962	$= £0.606$ per lb.
Revenue in 1970	$= £1.870$m.

---

11. It will be seen from Table V(a) that we obtain a relatively poor fit for the beer equation: the value of coefficient of determination was 0.575. It was, however, decided to use this equation for projection of beer consumption because of the lack of any better technique for projection. On the other hand, the figure obtained for beer consumption appears quite plausible in the light of past trends.

12. Tx/Y rose in 1963 because of substantial increases in excise tax rates on beer, sugar and cigarettes.

TABLE V (a)—(*continued*)

(4) *Revenue from tobacco:*
Tobacco consumption in 1970 = 450,000 lbs.
Tax rate in 1962   = £0.55 per lb.
Revenue in 1970   = £0.247m.

(5) *Revenue from other goods:*
(matches, spirits etc.)   = £0.075m.

Total excise tax revenue   = £4.818m.

Year			T_x/Y
1962	..	..	0.0269
1963	..	..	0.0289
1970	..	..	0.0239

TABLE V (b)

Projection of excise tax revenue under 6.6% growth rate

Here the value of $t = 16$, and $Y_d = 148.214$.

(1) *Revenue from beer:*
Projected beer consumption ('000 standard gallons) in 1970
                                            = 2888.624
Revenue from beer in 1970   = £0.979m.

(2) *Revenue from sugar:*
Projected sugar consumption ('000 cwt.) in 1970
                                            = 2292.244
Revenue from sugar in 1970   = £1.529m.

(3) *Revenue from cigarettes:*
Projected cigarettes consumption ('000 lbs) in 1970
                                            = 2894.673
Revenue from cigarettes in 1970 = £1.754m.
(4) Revenue from tobacco in 1970 = £0.247m.

(5) Revenue from other goods
     (matches, spirits etc.) in
     1970   = £0.065m.

Total excise tax revenue   = £4.574m.

T_x/Y in 1970   = 0.0254

price changes could have significantly affected the consumption of these commodities. Therefore, we are forced to the conclusion that excise taxes have an income elasticity of less than 1. This is rather surprising as beer, cigarettes and to a lesser extent sugar, are generally considered to have high income elasticities of demand.

4. Individual Income Tax

The projection of revenue from individual income tax is carried out in three stages. First we project the structural changes in the economy between 1962 and 1970 under the two alternative rates of growth. Secondly, we calculate the ratio of taxable income to gross product in each sector of the economy in a base year. Finally, on the basis of suitable assumptions about the average rate of taxation and the ratio of taxable income to sectoral gross product in 1970, we can calculate the individual income tax revenue in 1970.

Table I summarizes the structural changes in the economy implied by the Clark-Van Arkadie statistical growth model. It will be noticed that whether the economy grows at 8.2 per cent or 6.6 per cent p.a., all the sectors apart from agriculture and to a much lesser extent, transport, increase in relative importance[13]. Under 8.2 per cent growth rate, the share of agriculture falls from 46.4 per cent in 1962 to 40.4 per cent in 1970, while that of transport falls from 7.3 per cent to 7.0 per cent; the shares of construction, manufacturing, government and services rise from 3.6 per cent, 8.0 per cent, 11.5 per cent and 23.2 per cent to 6.2 per cent, 9.6 per cent, 12.4 per cent and 24.5 per cent respectively. Under a 6.6 per cent growth rate, the rise in the relative importance of construction and manufacturing is less marked, as also is the decline in the share of agriculture. The strategy of growth embodied in this model reflects a strong emphasis on construction and manufacturing.

The next step is to determine the ratio of personal taxable income to gross product in each sector. This was perhaps the most difficult part of the entire exercise. The details of the method employed are explained in the appendix to this chapter. We used the annual Income Tax Department Reports for the years 1961 and 1962 to derive the share of personal taxable income[14] in various sectors. The results are shown in Table VI (a). Several interesting conclusions emerge from a study of this table. Personal taxable income, as defined here, forms slightly less than 16 per cent of monetary G.D.P. The sectors with the highest ratios of taxable income to gross product are government (37.5%), services (27.7%)

---

13. The definitions of various sectors as used here are slightly different from those employed in G.D.P. tables in Uganda. Briefly, agriculture=agriculture, cotton ginning, coffee curing, sugar manufacture, forestry, fishing, hunting; manufacturing=mining, manufacture of food products, miscellaneous manufacturing; construction=construction; transport=transport, communications, electricity; services=commerce, private miscellaneous services, rents; government=government administration, public miscellaneous services, local government.

14. "Personal taxable income" as used here differs somewhat from the definition employed in the preceding chapters: in the first place, it excludes income from dividends, as the latter are included in corporate income; secondly, it is arrived at after deducting "interest and losses" from aggregate income of non-corporate bodies; we have not deducted "passage allowances, retirement benefit payments" etc.

TABLE VI (a)
Projection of individual income tax revenue to 1970[1]
1962

Sector	Taxable income[2] Gross Product	Taxable income £m.	Tax rate	Tax revenue £m.
Agriculture	0.017	0.762	0.090	0.069
Manufacturing	0.183	1.737	0.082	0.142
Construction	0.267	0.971	0.086	0.083
Transport	0.114	0.879	0.104	0.091
Services	0.277	7.169	0.088	0.631
Government	0.375	4.400	0.102	0.449
Pensions, interest etc.	0.008[3]	0.973	0.114	0.111
TOTAL	0.157	16.890	0.093	1.577

1970 at 8.2 per cent and 6.6 per cent P.A., growth rates[4]			
Agriculture	0.017	1.38	0.116	0.16
	0.017	1.28	0.108	0.14
Manufacturing ..	0.183	3.53	0.106	0.37
	0.183	2.69	0.098	0.26
Construction	0.267	3.34	0.111	0.37
	0.267	2.48	0.103	0.26
Transport	0.114	1.61	0.134	0.22
	0.114	1.40	0.125	0.18
Services	0.277	13.66	0.114	1.56
	0.277	12.02	0.106	1.27
Government	0.375	9.34	0.132	1.23
	0.375	9.34	0.122	1.14
Pensions, interest etc.	0.008[3]	1.61	0.147	0.24
	0.008	1.44	0.137	0.20
	0.171	34.47	0.120	4.15
	0.170	30.65	0.112	3.45

Notes: 1. For further details of these calculations, see Appendix II.
2. Average of taxable income/Gross Product ratios in 1961 and 1962.
3. Ratio of pensions, interest etc. to monetary G.D.P.
4. The upper line refers to 8.2 per cent growth rate and the lower line to 6.6 per cent.

construction (26.7%) and manufacturing (18.3%); while those with relatively low ratios are transport (11.4%); and agriculture (1.7%)[15]. It will be noticed that the sectors with relatively high ratios are also the ones which are expected to increase their share in income; while those with relatively low ratios are expected to decline in relative importance.

15. Our classification tends to over-estimate the share of taxable income in manufacturing and to underestimate it in agriculture, owing to the fact that some economic activities such as cotton ginning and coffee curing which are included in agricultural sector in our model have been subsumed under manufacturing in the Income Tax Department Reports. It has not been possible to obtain adequate information to correct this anomaly. However, this correction is unlikely to make much difference to the general picture.

The ratio of personal taxable income to gross product in each sector is determined by, *inter alia*, the labour intensity of the industry, the share of output from unincorporated enterprises in a given sector, the proportion of profits to gross outputs in such enterprises and, finally, by the relative importance of "high income" to "low income" persons among its labour force. The high ratios for government, services and construction are undoubtedly due to the labour intensive nature of these sectors and to the importance of unincorporated enterprises in services and construction, while the relatively low ratio for transport reflects a high degree of capital intensity as well as the relatively small importance of unincorporated enterprises in this sector. Agriculture is in a class by itself. Although it is highly labour intensive and largely unincorporated, it has a very low ratio of taxable income to gross product primarily because of the low per capita income in this sector, which results in an exemption of an overwhelming proportion of farmers from income tax assessment.

We next have to estimate the value of these ratios in 1970. It is difficult to decide as to what is the right assumption to make here. Clearly there are forces working in opposite directions. There will be a tendency for the ratio of taxable income to gross product to rise for a variety of reasons. The most important of these are an upward shift in all incomes due to rapid economic growth assumed in these projections and the even more rapid growth of money incomes. For both these reasons, individuals would tend to be shifted into higher income brackets, thereby increasing the number of persons subject to income tax. Furthermore, 1961 was the first year when Africans were subjected to income tax and it is likely that there is considerable underassessment of African taxable incomes. With the passage of time, there should be an improvement in the assessment of African incomes and hence an increase in the ratio of taxable income to gross product, especially in the agricultural and services sectors. There are, however, a number of considerations which would suggest a tendency for this ratio to decline. The most important of these relate to the position of non-Africans, especially Europeans, in the Uganda economy. In the past, the whole of income tax in Uganda had been paid by non-Africans, since Africans were exempted from income tax until 1961. With an expected decline in the share of non-African incomes, it is likely that the ratio of personal taxable income to monetary G.D.P. may decline. Furthermore, to the extent that the government is committed to pursuing policies designed to reduce inequalities in income and wealth, the proportion of persons with taxable income will tend to fall. It is of course impossible to state with any degree of confidence whether these factors will offset the ones noted earlier which have the effect of raising the ratio of taxable income to monetary G.D.P. There is the additional complication of uncertainty regarding the share of the incomes of unincorporated enterprises in different sectors. The aggregate ratios of taxable income to G.D.P. for the years 1958 to 1962, a period when there were no major changes in the structure of income tax, are fairly stable with a very slight upward trend; but then many of the factors which we have discussed above were not operative during that period. It is, therefore, not clear as to what extent the evidence of the past years may be taken as pointers to the future. In the circumstances, it appears most reasonable to assume that the 1961-62 sectoral ratios remain unchanged. However, even if the sectoral ratios remain constant, there will be a tendency for the over-all ratio to rise because of the relatively faster expansion of sectors with higher taxable income ratios. Table VI (a) shows that as a result of certain structural changes in the economy, the ratio of taxable income to monetary G.D.P. is projected to increase from 15.7 per cent in 1961-62 to 17.1 per cent in 1970 with an 8.2 per cent p.a. growth rate and to 17.0 per cent with a 6.6 per cent growth rate.

TABLE VI (b)
Individual income tax revenue relative to G.D.P.[1]

Year	Taxable income monetary G.D.P.	Average tax rate	Tax revenue monetary G.D.P.
1961	0.143	0.090	0.013
1962	0.157	0.093	0.015
1970 (8.2% growth) ..	0.171	0.120	0.021
1970 (6.6% growth) ..	0.170	0.112	0.019

Note: 1. The 1961-62 ratios differ from those shown in Table XI (a), Chapter III, owing to differences in the definition of Individual income tax base. For further details, see Appendix II.

The next step is to estimate the average rate of taxation on personal taxable income in 1970. We calculated the sectoral tax rates for 1962 on the basis of information contained in the Income Tax Department Report for 1962. These rates are shown in Table VI (a). It will be seen that the transport and government sectors have rates slightly higher than the average, while manufacturing, construction and services sectors have slightly lower rates. These sectoral tax rates are a function of the amount of allowances and deductions and pattern of income distribution within each sector.

The higher tax rates for transport and government appear to be due to lower proportion of allowances and deductions in these two sectors[16].

Once again it is difficult to decide on what basis to project these sectoral tax rates to 1970. With an unchanged pattern of income distribution among tax-payers, rapid economic growth may be expected to shift all tax-payers on to higher income groups, thereby pushing them into higher marginal tax brackets. As individual income tax in Uganda is steeply progressive, it is reasonable to expect an upward trend in the average tax rate. Empirical evidence bears this out: the average rate of individual income tax rose every year between 1958 and 1961, even though taxable incomes grew rather slowly. However, this effect of the progressive tax structure may, to some extent, be offset by a more even distribution of income among taxpayers, caused by a relative decline in non-African incomes and by a relatively more rapid expansion of the incomes of low income taxpayers[17]. Taking all these factors into account, we have assumed that with the economy growing at 8.2 per cent p.a., the overall average tax rate will rise from 9.3 per cent in 1962 to 12.0 per cent in 1970; the corresponding figure for 6.6 per cent p.a. growth rate has been assumed to be 11.2 per cent. We make the further assumption that in both cases, the sectoral tax rates will increase by the same proportion (29% and 20%) as the overall tax rate. The projected sectoral tax rates for 1970 are shown in Table VI (a).

Once we have made projections of taxable income and tax rates, it is easy to calculate the individual income tax revenue in 1970. The results of this calculation are shown in Table VI(a). It will be seen that revenue from individual income tax is projected to increase from £1.58m. in 1962 to £4.15m. and £3.45m. in 1970, depending on the rate of growth of the economy. Table VI(b) shows that tax revenue as a percentage of monetary G.D.P. is projected to rise from 1.5 per cent in 1962 to 2.1 per cent and 1.9 per cent in 1970, corresponding to the higher and lower growth rates of the economy. This increase is due to a combination of an increase in the ratio of taxable income to monetary G.D.P., caused

16. Allowances consist of single, marriage, children, life assurance allowances; while deductions are granted in respect of interest, losses, passage overseas, retirement benefit payments, alimony etc.

17. Another factor responsible for lowering the average rate of taxation between 1950 and 1956—the decline in the proportion of non-residents' to total taxable income—may be said to have worked itself out; the relative importance of non-residents' income has remained substantially unchanged between 1956 and 1962.

in the main by a more rapid expansion of sectors with higher taxable income ratios, and an increase in the average rate of taxation, caused primarily by the progressive nature of the income tax. We may, therefore, conclude that according to our projections, individual income tax emerges as highly income elastic.

5. *Corporate Tax*

We employ essentially the same method, as in the case of individual income tax, in order to make projections of revenue from corporate tax. There is, therefore, no need to discuss our method in detail. The first step, the projection of sectoral gross products in 1970, is attempted in Table I and was discussed in detail in the last section. Similarly, in order to calculate the sectoral taxable incomes[18], we had recourse to the Income Tax Department Reports for 1961 and 1962; the details of this calculation are explained in the Appendix to this chapter, and the results summarized in Table VII (*a*). It will be noticed that the aggregate ratio of corporate taxable income to monetary G.D.P. in 1961-62 was 5.5 per cent; the corresponding ratios for the individual sectors, however, show considerable diversity. At one extreme, we have the manufacturing sector where the ratio of taxable income to gross product is 35.2 per cent and at the other extreme the agricultural sector with a ratio of 0.3 per cent[19]. Transport and construction likewise have very low ratios of 2.9 per cent and 1.4 per cent respectively; the services sector comes somewhere in the middle with a taxable income ratio of 9.5 per cent. It will be noticed that apart from manufacturing the corporate sectoral taxable income ratios are substantially lower than the corresponding personal taxable income ratios.

Broadly speaking, the ratio of corporate taxable income to gross product will be determined by the share of the output of the incorporated enterprises in the sectoral gross product, the rate of profits and the degree of the capital intensity of the sector. It is thus easy to understand the relatively high ratio for the manufacturing sector where incorporation is the typical form of business

---

18. Corporate taxable income, as defined here, differs from the definition adopted in Chapter III, the main difference being that here corporate taxable income includes dividends paid out to shareholders, though not dividends received by one corporate body from another. In all other respects the two bases are identical i.e. they are both net of investment and depreciation allowances, and of "interest" and "losses". The definition employed here may, therefore, be interpreted as referring to total net profits, whereas in Chapter III we were concerned with undistributed profits.

19. However, see footnote 15, p. 104.

organization; moreover, manufacturing is a highly capital intensive industry. The low ratio for agriculture is due to its organization into numerous small peasants. If we study the non-African and public sector contribution to agriculture, the ratio rises to over 14 per cent. The transport sector, though highly capitalized, displays

TABLE VII (a)

Projection of corporate tax revenue to 1970[1]

1962

Sector		Taxable income:[2] Gross Product	Taxable income: £m.	Tax rate	Tax revenue: £m.
Agriculture	..	0.003	0.190	0.378	0.072
Manufacturing	..	0.352	2.769	0.378	1.047
Construction	..	0.014	0.100	0.375	0.038
Transport ..	..	0.029	0.204	0.375	0.076
Services ..	..	0.095	2.418	0.385	0.931
Government	..	—	—	—	—
Interest, other income etc.	..	0.0016[3]	0.171	0.373	0.064
Total	..	0.055	5.853	0.381	2.228

1970 at 8.2 per cent and 6.6 per cent P.A. growth rates[4]

Sector		Taxable income:[2] Gross Product	Taxable income: £m.	Tax rate	Tax revenue: £m.
Agriculture	..	0.003	0.24	0.378	0.09
		0.003	0.23	0.378	0.09
Manufacturing	..	0.352	6.79	0.378	2.57
		0.352	5.17	0.378	1.95
Construction	..	0.014	0.18	0.375	0.07
		0.014	0.13	0.375	0.05
Transport ..	..	0.029	0.41	0.375	0.15
		0.029	0.36	0.375	0.14
Services ..	..	0.095	4.68	0.385	1.80
		0.095	4.12	0.385	1.59
Government	..	—	—	—	—
		—	—	—	—
Interest, other income etc.	..	0.0016[3]	0.32	0.373	0.12
			0.29	0.373	0.11
Total	..	0.063	12.62	0.380	4.80
		0.057	10.30	0.382	3.93

Notes: 1. For further details of these calculations see Appendix II.
2. Average of taxable income/Gross product ratios for 1961 and 1962.
3. The ratio of interest, other income etc. to monetary G.D.P.
4. The upper line refers to 8.2 per cent growth rate and the lower line to 6.6 per cent.

a very low taxable income ratio; the reason for this is that the transport sector is dominated by a few large parastatal organizations such as the East African Railways and Harbours and the Uganda Electricity Board which have not been making any net profits in recent years. Finally, it comes as a surprise to find that the ratio of taxable income to gross product should be so low in the construction sector. There are several reasons for this. Firstly, a good deal of construction work is undertaken by the public sector which does not make any profits; secondly, construction is a highly labour intensive industry and therefore the share of profits in its gross product is likely to be low; thirdly, the construction industry has a large number of relatively small-sized unincorporated operators. Finally, construction has been a depressed industry during this period, resulting in low profit rates.

In order to make projections of corporate tax revenue, we have to make some assumption about the value of these sectoral ratios in 1970. Once again, in order to simplify our task, we shall assume that the 1961-62 ratios persist into 1970. This assumption implies that (a) the share of profits remains constant in each sector and (b) the share of the output from incorporated enterprises in the gross product of each sector remains constant. Although this is a simple assumption, it does not appear to be an unrealistic one, especially if we remember that changes in the share of profits and of incorporated enterprises in one sector may be offset by opposite changes in the other sectors. Table VII (a) shows that projecting taxable income on this basis results in an increase in the share of corporate taxable income in monetary G.D.P. from 5.5 per cent in 1961-62 to 6.3 per cent and 5.7 per cent in 1970, corresponding to 8.2 per cent and 6.6 per cent p.a. growth rates of the economy. This increase in the share of taxable income is due to the increase in the relative importance of manufacturing and services, both of which have relatively high taxable income ratios, and to a reduction in the share of agriculture—a sector with the lowest taxable income ratio.

The last step in our analysis is to project the average rate of taxation on corporate taxable income in 1970. This is a relatively simple matter, as the corporate tax is levied at a proportionate rate of $37\frac{1}{2}$ per cent. We have based our projections on the rates levied in 1962[20]. Table VII (a) shows that under the assumptions made here, corporate tax revenue has been projected to increase from £2.23m. in 1962 to £4.8m. and £3.93m. in 1970, corresponding to 8.2 per cent and 6.6 per cent p.a. growth rates of the economy. Table VII (b) further shows that the ratio of corporate tax revenue to monetary G.D.P. rises from 2.1 per cent in 1962 to 2.4 per cent and 2.2 per cent in 1970 according to whether the economy is

---

20. The slight divergences from $37\frac{1}{2}$ per cent tax rate are due to special provisions for certain types of businesses e.g. lower rate for mining companies as well as for trusts. There may also have been minor errors in classifying tax revenue under the categories adopted here.

assumed to achieve an 8.2 per cent or 6.6 per cent p.a. growth rate
respectively. As the tax rate is assumed to remain constant, this
increase in the ratio of tax revenue to G.D.P. is solely due to a
projected increase in the share of corporate taxable income in

TABLE VII (b)
Corporate tax revenue relative to G.D.P.[1]

Year	Taxable income monetary G.D.P.	Average tax rate	tax revenue monetary G.D.P.
1961	0.055	0.305	0.017
1962	0.054	0.381	0.021
1970 (8.2% growth) ..	0.063	0.380	0.024
1970 (6.6% growth) ..	0.057	0.382	0.022

Note: 1.   The 1961-62 ratios differ from those shown in Table XIII, Chapter III,
             owing to differences in the definition of corporate tax base. For
             further details, see Appendix II.

G.D.P. in 1970, which in turn is caused by a rise in the share of
manufacturing and services sectors in the economy, and a sharp
decline in the agricultural sector. The increase in the yield of corporate tax revenue relative to monetary G.D.P. would have been
even greater but for the fact that the construction sector, which is
projected to grow at the highest rate, has a very low ratio of corporate
taxable income to gross product. Nevertheless, according to our
projections, corporate tax emerges as possessing an income elasticity
greater than unity.

Before concluding this section, it may be of interest to calculate
the combined ratio of individual income and corporate tax revenue
to sectoral gross products. This is done in Table VIII, which shows
that this ratio is highest for manufacturing (13.8%), followed by
services (6.3%), government (3.6%), construction (3.1%), transport
(2.1%) and finally agriculture (0.3%)[21]. It will be noticed that
transport and agriculture are the two sectors which have been
projected to decline in relative importance in the growth model
used here; while the sectors with relatively high ratios are the ones
expected to increase their share in the economy. This is the main
reason why corporate and individual income tax emerge as income
elastic sources of revenue. Table VIII also shows that taxable
income forms well over 50 per cent of the manufacturing gross
product, followed by services (38.6%),   government (35.5%),
construction (28.2%), transport (14.1%) and agriculture (2.0%).

---

21. However, as indicated in footnote 15, p. 104, our method tends to over-
estimate the share of manufacturing and to underestimate the share of agriculture
by 1 per cent or so.

TABLE VIII

Individual and corporate tax revenue relative to G.D.P.

1962

Sector	Taxable income Sectoral Products	Tax rate	Tax Revenue Sectoral Products
Agriculture	0.020	0.148	0.003
Manufacturing	0.520	0.264	0.138
Construction	0.282	0.113	0.031
Transport	0.141	0.154	0.021
Services	0.386	0.163	0.063
Government	0.355	0.102	0.036
Interest, pensions etc. ..	0.023	0.153	—
Total	0.211	0.167	0.035

The manufacturing sector also has by far the highest tax rate (tax revenue/taxable income) at 26.4 per cent, followed by services (16.3%), transport (15.4%), agriculture (14.8%), construction (11.3%), and government (10.2%); this ranking is a reflection of, and is determined by, the relative importance of corporate income in different sectors, because of the much higher rate of corporate as compared with the individual income tax.

6. *Other Taxes*

Our last category consists of revenue from licences etc. Revenue from this source, which is relatively unimportant, was projected on the basis that it forms the same proportion of monetary G.D.P. in 1970 as in 1962. Table IX shows that revenue from other taxes is projected at £1.6m. if the economy grows at 8.2 per cent p.a., and at £1.4m. if it grows at the lower rate of 6.6 per cent p.a.

IV Conclusion

In this section we shall assess the income elasticity of the tax system as a whole. The relevant information is brought together in Table X, which shows the projected revenue from the main Central Government taxes in Uganda. It will be noticed that the total tax revenue is projected to increase from £17.31m. in 1962 (and £23.95m. in 1963) to £33.27m. and £31.24m. in 1970, according to whether the economy grows at 8.2 per cent or 6.6 per cent p.a. respectively. However, our interest is in total tax revenue (T) as a proportion of monetary G.D.P. (Y). Table X shows that according to our projections, with an unchanged 1962 tax structure, T/Y will rise from 16.1 per cent in 1962 to 16.5 per cent in 1970 if the economy grows at a rate of 8.2 per cent p.a.; T/Y will rise even more to 17.4

TABLE IX
Projection of revenue from other taxes
(licences etc.)

Year			T_L/Y	Tax revenue: £m.
1962	..	..	0.008	0.897
1963	..	..	0.007	0.947
1970 (8.2% growth rate)	..		0.008	1.611
1970 (6.6% growth rate)	..		0.008	1.440

TABLE X
Total tax revenue relative to G.D.P.[1]
£m.

Tax Source			1961	1962	1963	1970 (8.2% growth)	1970 (6.6% growth)
Import tax	..	..	6.32	7.18	9.24	11.65	11.81
Export duties		..	2.18	2.54	5.84	6.24	6.04
Excise duties	..		2.71	2.89	3.72	4.82	4.57
Income tax	..	..	3.32	3.80	4.20[2]	8.95	7.38
(individual +corporate)							
Licences, etc.		..	0.65	0.90	0.95	1.61	1.44
Total taxes (T)		..	15.18	17.31	23.95	33.27	31.24
Monetary G.D.P. (Y)			111.7	107.5	128.7	201.4	180.0
T/Y	..	..	0.1359	0.1610	0.1861	0.1652	0.1736

Notes: 1. The total tax revenue figures for 1961, 1962 and 1963 differ from those shown in Table I, Chapter 3, for two reasons: firstly, apart from export duties and licences, all revenue figures in this table relate to calender year, whereas in Table I (chapter 3) all these figures are derived by averaging revenue in two financial years. Secondly, the above table excludes revenue from estate tax and poll tax etc., which was quite substantial in 1961 and 1962.
2. Estimates made by the author.

per cent if the economy grows at the lower rate of 6.6 per cent p.a. It will also be noticed that T/Y in 1970 under both rates of growth will be lower than in 1963, when it was 18.6 per cent. On the other hand, there were several changes in import and excise tax rates in 1963 whose effect has been disregarded in our projections.

Before we conclude that the Uganda tax system is income elastic, even though very mildly, we need to bear in mind several qualifications. In the first place, 1962 was an exceptional year in that revenue from export taxes was at a very low level, partly because the cotton crop was half its normal size and partly because export prices for cotton and arabica coffee were the lowest since 1949. The second qualification refers to the assumptions made in projecting tax revenues. We have assumed a rather favourable price trend for coffee and may, therefore, have overestimated the likely revenue from export taxes. Similarly, our projection of individual income tax revenue probably errs on the higher side as well. For all these reasons our projections may appear to verge on the optimistic, and thus exaggerate the elasticity of the tax system.

However, assuming that our projections are "correct" and that the Uganda tax system is mildly income elastic under the growth path charted in the Clark-Van Arkadie statistical model, it is of some interest to analyse the changes in the relative importance of various taxes. According to our projections, compared with the base year 1962, import duties as well as excise taxes emerge as inelastic tax sources, while individual and corporate tax emerge as highly elastic. Export taxes are income elastic if the base year is 1962, but are inelastic if we treat 1963 as our base year. As in the past, the elasticity of the entire tax system will be vitally determined by the elasticity of export taxes. If the rather favourable trends assumed in our projections are realized, the Uganda tax system might well emerge as reasonably elastic. If, on the other hand, export price trends are less favourable than assumed here, export taxes would combine with import and excise taxes to damp down the elasticity of the tax structure to below unity.

APPENDIX II

Estimates of Sectoral Corporate and Personal Taxable Income Ratios and Tax Rates

Here we shall describe the method we used to obtain estimates of corporate and personal taxable income and tax revenue in individual sectors of the economy. Most of the information required to carry out this exercise was obtained from the East African Income Tax Department Reports for the years 1961 and 1962, supplemented by some unpublished material made available to the author. We calculated taxable income ratios for both 1961 and 1962. The ratios shown in Tables VI and VII are an average of sectoral ratios for 1961 and 1962.

The Income Tax Department Reports classify tax-payers into four categories: employees, individuals (partnerships and one-man firms), clubs, trusts etc. and companies. In our analysis, we have combined the first two categories into one—the individual income tax-payers, and the last two into another—the corporate tax-payers. This classification seems logical as employees and individuals are subject to a common individual income tax, while clubs, trusts and companies are subject to company income tax or to corporate tax, as we have called it here.

Our main difficulty arose from the fact that the sectoral classification adopted by the Income Tax Department (I.T.D.) Tables does not correspond exactly with the sectoral divisions of Gross Domestic Product tables, and *a fortiori*, with the classification adopted in our projection model. The I.T.D. Tables divide the income received by each type of tax-payer into the following sectoral categories: agriculture, mining, manufacture, construction, electricity and water etc., wholesale and retail trade, finance, real estate, transport and communications etc., services, and all others. For employees there is an additional category called Government and E.A.C.S.O. non-selfcontained services. Tax-payers are classified under the sectors from which they derive their main income. Income from each sector is then divided into the following categories: agriculture, trade, pension, employment, quarters, rents, dividends, interest untaxed, other income and averaging[1]. A simple example will clarify the I.T.D. scheme for classifying taxable incomes. Let us

---

1. Needless to say, pension and employment do not appear under the category "Companies, clubs, trusts etc."

assume that a businessman derives most of his income from manufacturing. He will, therefore, be classified under manufacturing and his income from manufacturing will be termed as income from "trade"; likewise the income he derives from dividends, rents, pensions, part-time employment etc. will be classified under these categories, though the aggregate income still appears under manufacturing.

Our task, therefore, reduced itself to reclassifying taxable income in accordance with the sectoral categories used in the projection model. Referring first to the I.T.D. sectoral classification, agriculture and construction coincided with their counterparts in our classification; mining and manufacturing were combined to form one category, corresponding to our category "manufacture"; likewise, transport and communications etc. and electricity and water were combined to form another category, corresponding to our category "transport"; lastly, wholesale and retail trade, finance, real estate, services and "all others" were combined to form one category, corresponding to our services sector. In order to obtain taxable income in the government sector, we assumed that nearly 80 per cent of the employees' income from "Government and E.A.C.S.O. non-self-contained services" could be attributed to the government sector. This figure was obtained on the basis of industrial classification of emoluments of non-Africans in the Public Services, contained in the "Enumeration of employees" for 1961 and 1962. The remaining 20 per cent of taxable income from "Government and E.A.C.S.O. non-self-contained services" was allocated to different sectors on the basis of information derived from the "Enumeration of employees" for 1961 and 1962.

Turning now to the various categories in which income from different sectors is classified, we have seen that the category "trade" refers to the income derived from the sector in question; income from the category "agriculture" was classified under the agriculture sector; income from quarters and rents was included in the services sector; income from employment was allocated to the sector under which it appears; finally, income from pension, interest untaxed, averaging and other sources, was subsumed under a new category called "pensions, interest untaxed etc.", as it was difficult to allocate them, even at a conceptual level, to any of the sectors of the projection model. This leaves us with income from dividends; it was decided to exclude dividend income from our definition of "taxable income" in order to avoid double-counting, as it is already included in corporate income.

Having thus classified aggregate taxable income into six

producing sectors of our projection model, we deducted "interest paid and losses" from each sector, thereby arriving at our tax bases—personal and corporate taxable incomes. It is to be noted that we have not deducted allowances given in respect of passages, retirement benefits, alimony or averaging. Having obtained taxable income in each sector, we divided them by sectoral gross products for 1961 and 1962 in order to derive taxable income ratios.

The second part of the exercise consisted in reclassifying tax revenue on the same lines as taxable income. The I.T.D. tables show the tax assessed by status i.e. employees, individuals, clubs and trusts, and companies, and also by sectors e.g. agriculture, mining, manufacture, construction etc. The first step in our analysis was to subtract the tax deducted at source on dividends income in each sector from the total tax assessed, in the same way as we had earlier deducted dividends from sectoral taxable income. This was quite simple as the tables give information on tax levied on dividends. Having obtained figures of net tax payable in each sector, we divided them by taxable incomes in the various sectors (I.T.D. classification) in order to estimate sectoral tax rates. We then adopted these tax rates for the various sectors in our projection model, after making the necessary adjustments. The difference between the actual tax payable and that obtained by applying these tax rates to the sectoral products in 1962 was deemed to be the tax assessed on income from "pensions, interest etc." The resulting tax rate confirmed the accuracy of our method of allocating tax revenue between different sectors of the economy.

Chapter VI

TOWARDS AN INCOME ELASTIC TAX STRUCTURE

I. Introduction

In the preceding chapter it was seen that even with rather optimistic assumptions about revenue from export and income taxes, the Uganda tax structure emerges as barely income elastic. This would indicate the need to move towards a more buoyant tax system in Uganda. The second five year plan in Uganda assumes very ambitious growth rates, in the fulfilment of which the public sector will have to play an increasingly important role. In order to facilitate this, a highly income elastic tax structure is a *sine qua non*. This can be seen by comparing projections of tax revenue and government expenditure. According to the projections made by Clark and Van Arkadie, current and capital government expenditure are assumed to rise by 7 per cent and 18.8 per cent p.a. respectively under an 8.2 per cent p.a. growth rate of the economy. Starting from £27.4m. and £4.9m. in 1962, this gives us a projection of £47.1m. and £19.4m. for current and capital expenditure respectively in 1970.[1]

It was seen in the last chapter that with an unchanged 1962 tax structure, our projection of tax revenue amounted to £33.3m. in 1970 under an 8.2 per cent p.a. growth rate of the economy. If we make allowance for post-1962 tax changes, the above figure is estimated to rise to about £36m. Inclusion of nonfiscal sources of revenue such as departmental earnings would raise this figure by about another £10m. to £46m. We, therefore, notice that the projected current revenue is barely adequate to cover current government expenditure. It is unrealistic to assume that the entire projected government investment of £19.4m. could be financed by borrowing from the public, the Central Bank or the overseas sources. A reasonable estimate would appear to be £2m. from the public, £2m. from the Central Bank and a further £5m. from abroad. This still leaves us with well over £10m. which would have to come from taxes. Thus in order to finance current, and a part of the capital, government expenditure, it will be necessary to raise

---

1. Preliminary estimates in the draft Second Five-Year Plan for Uganda, which assumes a similar growth rate of the economy, project capital expenditure, to about the same level as here, but recurrent expenditure is assumed to increase at a faster rate.

something like £47m. in taxes, which amounts to just over 23 per cent of projected monetary income in 1970. This can only be achieved by a comprehensive reform of the fiscal system in Uganda.

One way of raising additional revenue is to rely on *ad hoc* changes in tax rates and tax sources. This has been the practice in the last four to five years and will no doubt continue in the future. The recent changes in the tax structure represent an attempt to broaden the base of the tax system; these include the addition of soft drinks to excisable commodities, the imposition of higher duties on equipment and intermediate imports, and a reduction in single and marriage allowances. There are, however, some disadvantages in having to rely on continuous changes in tax rates and tax sources to raise additional revenue[2]. It would be preferable, if at all possible, to have a built-in flexibility in the tax structure, so that as incomes rise, revenue will increase by a greater proportion, thus facilitating an increasing role for the public sector in the economy. The main purpose of this chapter is to make specific proposals to enhance the income elasticity of the tax structure in Uganda. Although our proposals are made with respect to Uganda, they have a wider relevance since the tax structure of the three East African countries is essentially similar. It is further hoped that our proposals may have some relevance for other developing countries as well. One other point needs to be made: our proposals must satisfy the test of administrative feasibility and be not unacceptable on other economic grounds such as their effect on the allocation and growth of resources.

The tax structure may be made income elastic by securing progressivity of tax rates, expanding tax bases, and by the addition of new buoyant tax sources. The next three sections discuss the possibility of improving the flexibility of the Uganda tax system by each of these methods.

II. Increasing Income Elasticity of the Tax System

(i) *Operating on the Rates of the Existing Tax Sources*

One way of enhancing the income elasticity of a particular tax source is to make its rate structure progressive. It must, however, be emphasized that the rate must be made progressive with respect to the tax base and not any other variable. A simple example will illustrate this point. Export taxes in Uganda are progressive with respect to price increases but not with respect to quantity increases.

---

2. For an elaboration of this argument, see p. 4.

Therefore, the ratio of export taxes to value of cotton and coffee exports will rise only if the latter increases at least in part due to price increases; if export earnings rise solely because of an increase in the volume of exports, and in the face of constant or falling export prices, the tax rate will either stay constant or even decline. It will, therefore, be seen that according to this definition of a progressive tax rate, there are relatively few tax sources which possess a progressive tax structure. What is even more disturbing, there are few taxes which can possess a progressive rate structure in this sense. Of all the main taxes in Uganda, individual income tax is the only one which unambiguously possesses a progressive rate structure. This point will be clarified if we consider each of the main tax sources to see whether it is possible to impart progressivity to their rate structure.

→ note small labour force.

(a) Export Taxes

We have seen that in a period of rising export prices, the marginal rate of export taxes will exceed the average rate. If, on the other hand, the prices are expected to decline, the marginal rate will fall below the average rate. What is likely to be the trend in the export prices of cotton and coffee? It is of course impossible to predict primary product prices with any degree of certainty. In our projections of tax revenue, we assumed a declining price trend for cotton and a constant price for coffee at its 1963 level. But there are reasons to believe that we may have been optimistic in our assumption of constant coffee price. Certainly the short-term outlook at present does not seem too bright. It is, therefore, likely that both cotton and coffee prices may follow a downward trend.

Our next question, therefore, is: Can the tax rates be so structured as to make them progressive in the face of likely price declines? Tax rates may be related to three possible bases: prices, quantity or value of exports. If prices are expected to decline, the first possibility must be ruled out. The third possibility, i.e. relating tax rates to the value of exports is theoretically attractive but raises formidable administrative and equity problems. Export tax rate could be made progressive either with respect to aggregate export earnings or with respect to individual income from exports. In either case, taxes could only be collected in arrears, when the total value of exports of cotton and coffee or the incomes of individual farmers therefrom, were established. With considerable annual fluctuations in individual as well as aggregate earnings from cotton and coffee exports, assessment and collection of taxes in arrears would be a source of great hardship and inequity. In any case, an assessment of individual farmers' incomes would pose insuperable administrative problems and must therefore be rejected on grounds of administrative feasibility. Furthermore, this proposal would amount to a progressive income tax on export incomes only, and would appear to be inferior to a general income tax embracing income from all sources.

The difficulty with using the aggregate value of cotton and coffee exports as a base for export taxes is that it ignores completely the export incomes of individual farmers and with rising export earnings will mean high marginal tax rates on all farmers irrespective of their export income. It will thus impose great hardship on un-fortunate farmers whose output stays constant or actually declines while the total value of exports experiences a sharp increase. We must, therefore, reject export earnings as a base for export tax.

We are thus left with the second possibility i.e. relating tax rate to the quantity exported. In a period of declining prices, a specific export tax will ensure a rising tax rate and contribute to the enhancement of the income elasticity of export taxes. More-over, it is one of the simplest taxes to administer. One of the dis-advantages of this proposal is that it will not have a stabilizing effect on the economy; in particular, in boom periods the economy may be subjected to considerable inflationary pressures in the absence of an export tax related to prices. Furthermore, it may be argued that in periods of very low prices, a specific export tax will bear unduly hard on producers. This argument may not hold if productivity and, therefore, the volume of exports were to increase rapidly and equally for all farmers. There is the further difficult problem with this proposal of determining the rate of duty per unit of export. Despite these difficulties, a fixed tax per unit of export is the only practicable way of assuring a progressive rate in the event of a gradual decline in export prices[3]. We, however, feel that on the whole its deficiencies from the point of view of equity and stabilization are so serious as to outweigh its revenue advantages and for this reason we hesitate to recommend this proposal for adoption. In the event, the least disadvantageous export tax would appear to be the one relating tax rates to export prices. This,

---

3. It is further possible to improve the stability of export tax revenue through a composite export tax—a given tax per unit of export plus a tax related to price. This would make the tax less inelastic in the face of price declines but quantity increases—a situation that is envisaged here. I am indebted to Dr. C. R. Frank for this point.

however, does not mean that the present tax rate schedules on cotton and coffee are entirely satisfactory. We have seen that under the present tax schedule, cotton producers have been taxed far more heavily than coffee growers. In view of the existence of quotas on coffee exports, it would be a sound economic policy as well as more equitable to lower the coffee price floor to its pre-1965 level of £90 per ton f.o.b. Mombasa for Robusta coffee.

(b) Import Taxes

It was seen earlier that the average rate of import duties may decline over time as a result of two factors: firstly, because of the expected changes in the composition of imports, and secondly because some of the duties are levied on a specific rather than *ad valorem* basis; this will result in a decline in average tax rates in a period of rising prices. By the same token, there are two ways in which the decline in average rates can be moderated: firstly, by the conversion of specific into *ad valorem* rates, and secondly, by altering the pattern of import duties in such a way as to impose higher rates on imports which are expected to increase in relative importance. This in effect implies higher rates on construction materials, machinery and equipment and intermediate products. This proposal goes against the traditional practice in Uganda of admitting capital good imports either duty-free or at very low rates. Its main disadvantage is that it will make capital goods more expensive and hence may have disincentive effects on capital formation. It is, of course, not possible to say without a great deal of investigation how serious these adverse effects may turn out to be. Such costs will have to be weighed against the expected benefits from larger tax revenue. One beneficial by-product of the proposed changes in the pattern of import duties will be a stimulus to labour-intensive techniques of production—a thoroughly desirable effect in an economy where there is considerable urban unemployment, alleged to have been caused in part by a progressive substitution of capital for labour, which in turn has resulted from a rapid rise in wage rates. There are, however, strict limits to the level to which import duties on producers' goods can be raised. Even if the two proposals mentioned here are implemented, the best that can be hoped for is moderation of the decline in import tax rates, rather than a reversal of the direction of change, unless of course import duties on producers' goods are to be raised to uneconomically high levels. Apart from this, there appears to be some scope for restructuring import duty rates on luxury and semi-luxury goods in such a way as to impose relatively higher duties on goods with a high income elasticity of demand and which are unlikely to be produced domestically over the next decade or so.

(c) Excise Duties

We need not spend much time on a discussion of excise duty rates, as the analysis developed in the preceding section applies here. At the moment, all excise duties are levied on a specific basis; with an upward trend in the prices of excisable goods, the average rate will tend to decline. In order to prevent this decline, it is necessary to convert the specific into *ad valorem* rates. This might prove administratively more difficult, but the difference will only be a marginal one. As with import duties, the other method of imparting an upward bias to the average tax rate is to levy relatively higher rates on commodities with a relatively high elasticity of demand. Of the main excisable commodities, our projections showed that the consumption of sugar is expected to increase most, followed by beer, cigarettes and tobacco[4]. Therefore, relatively higher rates on beer and sugar will impart on upward bias to average excise duty rates, and hence improve the income elasticity of excise taxes.

(d) Corporate Tax

As in most other countries, corporate tax in Uganda is levied at a proportionate rate. It is, of course, possible to levy a progressive tax rate on the income of companies, on the same lines as individual income tax; but corporate incomes are hardly ever subject to a progressive tax. The main reasons for this are administrative inconvenience, possibilities of evasion through break-up of integrated industries, and disincentive effects on efficient, enterprising firms. Also, if the corporate tax is not shifted, shareholders will bear corporate tax at erratic rates on undistributed profits. Besides, the usual rate on corporate income is fairly high, ranging from 35 per cent to 55 per cent in most countries; in order to raise the same amount of revenue from progressive tax, the rates

---

4.

	Consumption in 1963	Projected consumption in 1970
Beer ('000 standard gallons)	1,885.894	2,976.712
Sugar ('000 cwt)	1,506.196	2,435.369
Cigarettes ('000 lbs)	2,308.731	3,086.299

It will thus be seen that sugar consumption is projected to rise by 62 per cent, beer by 58 per cent and cigarettes by 34 per cent. Our projections were made on the assumption that the economy grows at a rate of 8.2 per cent p.a., and the regression equation was obtained on the basis of data for the period 1954-63. If we compare consumption figures over a longer period, beer appears to have experienced the greatest relative increase.

will have to be very steeply progressive. For all these reasons, it is preferable to levy corporate tax at a proportionate rate. Corporate tax will, therefore, be income elastic only if corporate income increases its share in national income.

(e) Individual Income Tax

Individual income tax already embodies a steeply progressive rate structure. But even with a progressive tax structure, the pattern of distribution of incremental income will determine whether the marginal rate will exceed the average rate. The accrual of additional income to persons who are liable to marginal rates of taxation less than the average rate on the total taxable income will have the effect of lowering the average rate of taxation. In general, we may say that if the weighted average of the marginal tax rates payable by individuals receiving additional income exceeds the original average rate, the tax will tend to be income elastic. The policy implication of this is clear: a policy favouring increasing inequalities of income is most conducive to revenue maximization. But it is also clear that revenue maximization is only one of the goals of public policy and in this particular instance, it may have to be sacrificed in the interests of an even more important objective—the achievement of an egalitarian society.

To round off our discussion of tax rates, we may conclude that it is rather difficult to devise progressive rates for most of the taxes under consideration, and therefore an automatic increase in tax rates may be expected to contribute little, if at all, to the enhancement of the elasticity of tax structure in Uganda. If a high proportion of the tax revenue were to accrue from individual income tax and/or from a progressive expenditure tax of the type advocated by Kaldor[5], the progressive structure of tax rates could make a powerful contribution towards the flexibility of the fiscal system. But in Uganda where direct taxes on income are relatively unimportant and most of the revenue is derived from indirect taxes like export, import and excise taxes, the scope for manipulating tax rates to increase the income elasticity of tax structure is rather limited. The strategy for revenue maximization over time must concentrate on structuring indirect taxes in such a way as to levy higher rates on goods and services with a high income elasticity of demand.

---

5. N. Kaldor, *An Expenditure Tax* (George Allen and Unwin Ltd., London, 1955).

(ii) *Operating on the Bases of Existing Tax Sources*

Assuming a constant average tax rate, a tax may still be income elastic provided the share of its base in national income shows an upward trend. The bases for most of the taxes under consideration here are either some component of income or of expenditure. The former is true of export duties, individual and corporate income tax while the latter holds for import and excise duties. We shall discuss each of these taxes in turn.

(a) *Export Taxes*

At the moment export taxes are levied only on exports of cotton, coffee and hides and skins. The export tax base can be broadened by bringing within its net a number of other agricultural exports such as animal feeding stuffs, tea, groundnuts, castor seed etc. Even low rates of export duties on such products will bring in considerable sums of revenue. Economists are generally opposed to export taxes: they are alleged to be discriminatory, disincentive, and a highly fluctuating source of revenue[6]. Undoubtedly there is much truth in these criticisms, though it has hardly ever been shown satisfactorily that export taxes have disincentive effects. This is a complex subject and will take us away from our main theme. We shall not, therefore, pursue it further here, except to say that with all their alleged disadvantages, there is no really practicable alternative to export taxes. They are cheap and simple to administer, and are a very convenient way of raising large sums of money from numerous small-scale peasants who constitute the overwhelming proportion of working population in these countries. It is most unlikely that governments would be able to raise such large sums of revenue through reliance on other taxes. Those who condemn export taxes must weigh their disadvantages either against the benefits derived from the public expenditure of proceeds from these taxes, or against the economic costs of raising similar amounts

---

6. *Report of the Uganda Fiscal Commission, op. cit.*, pars. 83–85, J. F. Due, *Taxation and Economic Development in Tropical Africa, op. cit.*, p.98; United Nations, *Taxes and Fiscal Policy in Underdeveloped Countries, op. cit.*, p. 40; P. T. Bauer and B. S. Yamey, *The Economics of Underdeveloped Countries* (Nisbet and Cambridge University Press, Cambridge, 1957) ch. XIII; R. Nurkse, "Trade Fluctuations and Buffer Policies of Low Income Countries," *op. cit*; Prest, *Public Finance in Underdeveloped Countries, op. cit.*, pp. 66–69. For a different viewpoint, nearer to the one taken in this study, see R. H. Green, "Ghana Cocoa Marketing Policy, 1938–1960," *Conference Proceedings*, Nigerian Institute of Social and Economic Research, Ibadan, 1962; and G. K. Helleiner, "The Fiscal Role of the Marketing Boards in Nigerian Economic Development, 1947–61," *The Economic Journal* (September, 1964).

of revenue from other taxes. Needless to say, no one has carried
out this sort of analysis. The need for additional revenue is so great
in most developing countries that very few governments can afford
to neglect export taxes in their search for revenue. This is our
justification for proposing an extension of export taxes to cover
other agricultural exports. Apart from broadening the base of
export taxes, our proposal will make the current tax system less
discriminatory by applying these taxes to all primary product
exports, and reduce the alleged distortion of allocation of
resources.

(b) Import Taxes

There is little that can be done to widen the import base, apart
from imposing import duties on inter-territorial imports. But this
raises many other complicated issues relating to the East African
Common Market which are irrelevant to our problem and will not,
therefore, be pursued further.

(c) Excise Taxes

The base of excise taxes can only be broadened by bringing
new products within its scope. This aspect of tax reform will be
dealt with in the next section.

(d) Corporate Tax

We have seen earlier that the share of corporate income in
national income is likely to increase over time. There is another
way in which the base for corporate tax can be increased: by
elimination or reduction of investment and accelerated depreciation
allowances. The benefits of additional tax revenue from this change
will have to be weighed against the stimulus to investment given
by such concessions. If these allowances have a powerful effect
on the volume of investment, then clearly the present concessions
must continue. If, on the other hand, their effect on investment is
only marginal, consideration must be given to reducing some of
these allowances in order to increase tax revenue. As with so many
economic problems, it is not possible to say, without much further
investigation, how important these tax concessions are in stimulating
investment. The authorities will also have to bear in mind the effect of
such concessions on techniques of production, and consequently
on the level of unemployment.

Corporate tax base can be broadened further by encouraging
the conversion of unincorporated into corporate enterprises
through a variety of non-fiscal concessions. The former are subject

to individual income tax; but as we have seen, the average tax rate on corporate income is substantially in excess of that on personal income. Thus the conversion of unincorporated into corporate enterprises will result in a substantial increase in tax revenues.

(e) *Individual Income Tax*

We have seen earlier that personal taxable income is likely to increase its relative importance over time. There are further possibilities of increasing the share of personal taxable income in G.D.P. and making it more income elastic. Introduction of P.A.Y.E. is a badly needed reform; it can be expected to bring about an improvement in coverage and assessment, at the same time eliminate the time lag between the receipt of income and collection of income tax. This proposal would have the effect of increasing once-for-all the ratio of personal taxable income to G.D.P.; it will also improve the flexibility and stabilizing quality of the tax system by relating tax revenue to current rather than to the past income.

Another reform which would result in a considerable once-for-all increase in the tax base is reduction of single and marriage allowances. We have seen that only recently marriage and single allowances were reduced from £700 and £225 to £600 and £216 respectively. It would seem reasonable to reduce them still further to £400 and £200 respectively. This would greatly increase the number of income tax payers and with increasing incomes will make the tax base highly elastic. Further, pursuit of policies designed to enhance or at least to perpetuate existing income inequalities will tend to increase the share of taxable incomes in G.D.P. Finally, a progressive improvement in coverage and assessment would introduce another factor contributing to the increase of the share of tax base in G.D.P. It is widely believed that there is considerable tax evasion by businessmen and independent professionals. A tightening up of tax assessment would, therefore, be an important step in the direction of making the tax system more equitable as well as more buoyant.

(iii) *Introduction of New Tax Sources*

With the reforms we have proposed above, the flexibility of taxes on income will be considerably enhanced. There does not appear to be further substantial scope for additional taxes on income, or for raising additional revenue from the existing taxes on income. The elasticity of the tax system must somehow be strengthened by the inclusion of appropriate consumption-based taxes in the fiscal armoury. One of the most important gaps in the present tax structure is the failure to tax adequately either the production or consumption of domestically produced goods and services. This gap is especially serious as domestically produced goods and services are likely to be a very rapidly expanding base.

A progressive expenditure tax along the lines proposed by Kaldor could be a highly income elastic tax, but it has to be rejected on grounds of administrative feasibility. Two possibilities remain (i) a general sales tax levied at the wholesale stage, as it is not practicable to levy it at the retail level under the existing conditions in Uganda; (ii) A purchase, excise or wholesale tax on selected goods and services; and of course a combination of (i) and (ii).

(i) Few of the sales taxes are really general; most of them exempt basic necessities and producers' goods. If a sales tax on semi-necessities and luxuries is levied at the wholesale stage, the tax base will prove fairly buoyant, as the ratio of consumption of semi-necessities and luxuries to national income might be expected to increase over time with the improvement in the standard of living of the masses. A wholesale tax could in the first instance be levied at a relatively low rate, say at 5 per cent, and be increased later as the need arose.

(ii) A selective indirect tax at a relatively high rate on goods and services which have a high income and low price elasticity of demand will also contribute significantly to the flexibility of the entire tax system. Services are hardly taxed in Uganda at the moment; yet in many respects they are ideal 'commodities' for tax purposes: most of them are consumed by the wealthier members of the society, have high income elasticity of demand and do not pose any great administrative problems. A lot more work needs to be done to determine the income and price elasticities of demand for various goods and services. But it is clear even at this stage that services like hotels, various forms of entertainment, travel, education, catering, electricity, etc. have high income elasticity of demand and could form suitable objects of taxation. Likewise, goods such as textiles, clothing, household effects, bicycles, transistors etc. are generally considered to have a high income elasticity of demand. Inclusion of goods and services of this kind in consumption-based taxes, either by themselves or in addition to a low rate general sales tax, could greatly strengthen the flexibility of the entire tax structure and ensure adequate revenue for the expansion of the public sector.

III Conclusion

By their very nature, most taxes cannot have a progressive

rate structure. We have seen that individual income tax is the only truly progressive tax in Uganda, and that export taxes may become progressive if export earnings rise at least in part due to an increase in the export prices of cotton and coffee. We have made some proposals whose effect will be to enhance the progressivity of tax rates for certain tax sources. But the more promising avenue to increase the income elasticity of the entire tax system is to operate through the tax bases. Apart from increased reliance on taxes on income, the basic strategy should be to choose expanding tax bases for indirect taxes. We have made several proposals to bring about this result. If they are implemented, the effect will be to greatly improve the flexibility of tax structure and to obviate the necessity of continuous changes in tax rates and tax bases to raise more revenue. Owing to lack of adequate statistical data, it has not been possible to give quantitative estimates of the increase in revenue to be expected from the implementation of the proposals outlined above. However, once the necessary data become available, it should not prove difficult to translate the qualitative proposals into their quantitative equivalents.

The above agenda for tax reform can be criticized only too easily on grounds of incentives or administrative feasibility. But it has been proposed in the firm conviction that lack of adequate revenue is a crucial constraint on the development of many developing countries and the elimination of this constraint will open up possibilities of higher growth rates.

Selected Bibliography

Only those publications which have a direct bearing on the theme of our study will be mentioned here. No attempt is being made to list all the material that was consulted by the author in the course of this study.

BOOKS AND ARTICLES

Bretherton, R. F.	"The Sensitivity of Taxes to Fluctuations of Trade", *Econometrica*, (1937).
Cary Brown, E. and Kruizenga, R. J.	"Income Sensitivity of a Simple Personal Income Tax", *Review of Economics and Statistics*, (August 1959).
Cary Brown, E.	"The Static Theory of Automatic Fiscal stabilization", *Journal of Political Economy* (1955).
Chelliah, R. J.	*Fiscal Policy in Underdeveloped Countries* (George Allen and Unwin, London, 1960).
Clark, J. M.	"Export Taxes on Tropical Products", *Monthly Bulletin of Agricultural Economics*, (F.A.O. May, 1963).
Clark, P. G.	*Development Planning in East Africa* (East African Publishing House, 1965).
Cohen, L. J.	"An Empirical Measurement of the Built-in Flexibility of the Individual Income Tax", *American Economic Review* (May, 1959).
Cohen, L. J.	"A More Recent Measurement of the Built-in Flexibility of the Individual Income Tax", *National Tax Journal* (1960).
Due, J. F.	*Taxation and Economic Development in Tropical Africa* (M.I.T. Press, Massachusetts, 1963).
Due, J. F. and Robson, P.	"Tax Harmonization in the East African Common Markets", in *"Tax Harmonization in Common Markets"*, edited by C. Shoup (Columbia University Press, forthcoming).
Dosser, D. and Peacock, A. T.	"Stabilization and Economic Planning in African Countries", *Public Finance:* No. 3 (1962).

Economic Development Research Project Papers by P. G. Clark, B. Van Arkadie, D. P. Ghai, C. R. Frank, Y. Kyesimira, (East African Institute of Social Research, 1964) mimeo.

Edelberg, V.	"Flexibility of the Yield of Taxation—Some Econometric Investigations", *Journal of the Royal Statistical Society* (1940).
Gill, P. J.	"The Future of Taxation Policy in an Independent East Africa", *East African Economic Review*, (June 1962).
Goode, R.	"Taxation and Economic Development", reprinted in *"Readings in Economic Development"*, edited by J. Morgan, G. W. Bitz and N. K. Choudhry.
Heller, J. and Kauffman, K. M.	*"Tax Incentives for Industry in Less Developed Countries"*, (Harvard University Press, Cambridge, 1963).

Hicks, U.K. .. .. .. *Development From Below* (Oxford University Press, 1961).

Kaldor, N. .. .. .. *An Expenditure Tax* (George Allen and Unwin, London, 1955).

Kaldor, N. .. .. .. *Indian Tax Reform* (Ministry of Finance, Government of India, 1956).

Kaldor, N. .. .. .. "Taxation and Economic Development", *Journal of Modern African Studies* (1963).

Martin, A. and Lewis, A. W. "Patterns of Public Revenue and Expenditure", *Manchester School*, (September, 1956).

Musgrave, R. A. and Miller .. "Built-in Flexibility", *American Economic Review* (1948).

Musgrave, R. A. .. .. *Theory of Public Finance* (McGraw-Hill Inc., New York, 1959).

Nurkse, R. .. .. .. "Trade Fluctuations and Buffer Policies of Low-income Countries", *Kyklos* (Vol. 11, 1958).

Nuruddin Chowdhury A. H. M. "The Predictability and the Flexibility of Tax Revenue in Pakistan", *The Pakistan Development Review* (Vol. III, 1963).

Peacock, A. T. .. .. "Fiscal Policy Problems in African Countries" in *Economic Development in Africa*, editor, E.A.G. Robinson.

Pechman, J. A. .. .. "Yield of the Individual Income Tax During a Recession", *Policies to Combat Depression*, National Bureau of Economic Research (Princeton University Press, 1956).

Prest, A. R. .. .. .. *Public Finance* (Wiedenfeld and Nicolson, London, 1960).

Prest, A. R. .. .. .. *Public Finance in Underdeveloped Countries* (Wiedenfeld and Nicolson, London, 1963).

Prest, A. R. .. .. .. "The Sensitivity of the Yield of Personal Income Tax in the U.K.", *Economic Journal* (Sept. 1962).

Sahota, G. S. .. .. .. *Indian Tax Structure and Economic Development*, (Asia Publishing House, Bombay, 1961).

Smyth, D. J. .. .. .. "Can Automatic Stabilizers be Destabilizing?" *Public Finance*, No. 3 (1963).

Tripathy, R. N. .. .. *Public Finance in Underdeveloped Countries* (World Press Private Ltd., Calcutta, 1964).

Walker, D. .. .. .. "Income Taxes on Africans in Uganda", *East African Economic Review* (1959).

Walker, D. .. .. .. "A Recent Change in East African Company Taxation", *Public Finance* (1960).

OFFICIAL PUBLICATIONS

Background to the Budget (Annual); 1956-65. (Government Printer, Entebbe).

Report on a Fiscal Survey of Kenya, Uganda and Tanganyika, Sir Wilfred Woods, (Government Printer, Nairobi, 1946).

Report of the East African Commission of Inquiry on Income Tax (Government Printer, 1958).

Report on Economic and Fiscal Commission: East Africa, cmnd. 1279 (H.M.S.O. London, 1961).

Report of the Taxation Enquiry Committee, 1947 (Government Printer, Nairobi, 1948).

Report of the Income Tax Committee, Kenya, 1953-54 (Government Printer, Nairobi, 1955).

Report of the Uganda Fiscal Commission (Government Printer, Entebbe, 1962).

Report of the East African Income Tax Department: annual since 1948.

Trade Reports, East Africa High Commission and East African Common Services Organization: annual since 1948.

Statistical Abstracts, Uganda: annual since 1955 (Government Printer, Entebbe).

Published by East African Publishing House Ltd., P.O. Box 30571, Uniafric House, Koinange Street Nairobi and Printed by Kenya Litho Ltd., Cardiff Road, P.O. Box 775, Nairobi.

EAST AFRICAN PUBLISHING HOUSE

EAST AFRICAN INSTITUTE OF SOCIAL RESEARCH

Everyone wants development. Governments have to find the money for it. Dharam Ghai has made an important contribution to the scarce literature on public finance in developing countries with this book. It is a first-rate analysis of past taxation policy in Uganda and contains many projections for the future which will be of great interest to policy makers.

Cover Design by Frank Horley

20/- *in East Africa*